"A distinctive book, emphasizing the presence of the Goddess in daily life. From power and peace rituals to blessings for our children and foremothers, this down-to-earth guide is for all who seek to connect with the sacred Goddess." — *Moving Words*

"A delightful and down-to-earth excursion into realms mystical and magical. A do-it-yourself class in basic ritual that sings with the love of the Goddess." —Anodea Judith, author, *The Sevenfold Journey: Reclaiming Mind, Body & Spirit Through the Chakras*

"A very readable little book full of wonderful information, insights, and wisdom; well-written, well-produced. An excellent book for any-one wanting to discover and know the Goddess who is all around us." —Cristina Biaggi, author *Habitations of the Great Goddess*

"In this lush book of rituals and celebrations, voiced in beautifully po-etic language, Barbara Ardinger presents to us a multiplicity of ways to go 'between the worlds': to honor ourselves, our female ancestors, our children, our Mother Earth, and the Great Round which makes up the seasons of our world. As a lover of the ancient ways, I particularly enjoyed 'A Blessing for Our Foremothers': an honoring of our moth-ers, grandmothers, great-great-grandmothers, 'heras,' divine women: all those women—historic and prehistoric—who, having been inter-woven into the fabric of our lives, have contributed to who we are. As we honor our female line, so we honor ourselves at our very founda-tions, and so we re-form spiritual foundations for our own lives." —Miriam Robbins Dexter, Ph.D., author *Whence the Goddesses: A Source Book*

"A journey into the world of Goddess Thealogy and practice that will positively change your life . . . without asking you to make any radi-cal changes in your present lifestyle." — Gloria Feman Orenstein author of *The Reflowering of the Goddess*

"In this wonderfully down-to-earth book on the how and why of God-dess rituals, author and Witch Barbara Ardinger shows us how to bring rituals and the Goddess into our lives in the most basic ways. The author's writing is laced with a wonderful sense of humor that undercuts what might sound like preachy dogma in the hands of a less-skilled writer. This is the best general book on designing rituals I've seen to date. The balance of theory with examples and ideas is just right, resulting in a well-written, user-friendly volume that is suit-able for any woman interested in Goddess spirituality or Witchcraft." — *Whole Life Times*

A WOMAN'S BOOK OF

RITUALS &

CELEBRATIONS

Revised Edition

BARBARA ARDINGER, PH.D.

NEW WORLD LIBRARY
NOVATO, CALIFORNIA

New World Library
14 Pamaron Way
Novato, CA 94949

© 1995 by Barbara Ardinger, Ph.D.

Cover design: Kathy Warinner
Text design: Stephanie Young
Composition: Stephanie Eichleay
Word Processing: Deborah Eaglebarger

Library of Congress Cataloging-in-Publication Data

Ardinger, Barbara, 1941–
A woman's book of rituals and celebrations /
by Barbara Ardinger.
p.   cm.
Includes bibliographical references.
ISBN 1-880032-57-0 (acid free paper)
1. Women — Religious life. 2. Goddess religion — Rituals.
3. Goddess religion — Prayer-books and devotions — English.
4. Devotional calendars. 5. Ritual. I. Title.

BL625.7.A55 1992   91-4162
291.3'8'082 — dc20   CIP

ISBN 1-880032-57-0
Second edition, 1995
Distributed by Publishers Group West
10 9 8 7 6 5 4 3 2

DEDICATION

First, as always to my son, Charles Ardinger. He's a true blessing in my life. Then to all the Goddess's children — women, men, kids, cats, snakes, and flowers — that I've met at rituals and who have enriched my life. We've danced, drummed, sung, talked, and giggled together. We've worshipped and played together at large and small, planned and spontaneous rituals, and we've learned what the practice of the presence of the Goddess really is.

ACKNOWLEDGMENTS

My good friends Gloria Feman Orenstein, Elder High Priestess Marsha Smith Shaw, and Clarissa Ingabetsen have given me hours of wonderful conversation, good ideas, and endless support. I've also done some extraordinary rituals with them.

My literary agent, Judy Semler, works hard on my behalf and is a true friend besides.

Special thanks to Marc Allen, President of New World Library. We have wonderful phone conversations. In April 1994, he phoned to say they were re-releasing this book. Six months later, he phoned to say I could rewrite it. That meant I could correct my mistakes and (no doubt) make a few new ones. It's good to have a publisher who admires and supports my work and I'm grateful to be working with Marc and his staff.

When you write books, you find out who your *real* friends are. They're the ones who return your phone calls, whose eyes don't glaze over when you lecture them about your research, who sympathize when you sputter on about the vagaries of software and publishers, who go, "There, there, it's all right" when you just sit and stare. My most patient friends are Sandra Caton, Patricia Kelly, Barbara Pogosian, Rose Sheppard, Arlene Solomon, Marilyn Spivey, and Suzan Walter. Their help on this book, while indirect, has been priceless.

FOREWORD

Dear Reader, Congratulations on your fine literary taste, and on your keen psychic sensitivity! If Barbara Ardinger's excellent and extremely user-friendly book on women's rituals and celebrations has called out to you today, it is certainly because you are someone for whom the time has now come to connect with the creative cosmic energy here identified as that of the Goddess.

Undoubtedly you have already absorbed enough information about the importance of reclaiming the Goddess (and the ecofeminist values She both embodies and personifies) in our world to be ready to take the next step, that of learning to incorporate the Path of the Goddess into your personal life. It is not by chance that you have begun to read this book now. On the contrary, if this book has drawn you to read this far, it is obviously because you are ready to move forward in your response to the life-affirming message of Goddess spirituality. Since this is the case, I am pleased to announce that there is one thing I can absolutely guarantee. I can promise you a journey into the world of Goddess Thealogy and practice that *will* positively change your life (while also increasing the quantity and quality of Light in the world) without asking you to make any radical changes in your present lifestyle.

Practicing the Presence of The Goddess is no harder than cooking a fine meal, according to Barbara Ardinger. She will personally guide and direct you in how to transform the simple, everyday objects in your home and the seemingly ordinary events of your life into powerful ritual tools and into sacred moments of Goddess revelation.

Barbara is both a literary scholar and a practitioner of Wicca (a Priestess or a Witch), but one of a very "down home" variety—as all the genuine "Wise Women" of the past have always been. She has written a book that is scholarly as well as practical. She encourages you to make Magic happen in your own life by using whatever is available and meaningful to you. Barbara provides the step-by-step instructions, showing you how to produce the magical effects of "abracadabra" in any area of life's journey that you choose to illuminate with the radiance of the teachings of the Goddess.

Your daily acts make a huge difference in our world. Perhaps you have never thought of yourself in that way before. If not, this book will show you how *who you are, what you believe, and what you do matters*, and how it affects everything in the universe from a grain of sand to the fate of nations. If, as the Goddess teaches, everything is interconnected, then the way you live your life may just create the ripple that grows into the wave that may turn the tide in the course of the history of life on Earth.

Your desire to heal Mother Earth now that She is ailing and your prayers for peace, balance, and harmony in the world have been received. You have been "called" to become a vital part of the solution, to become both the "changer" and the "changed." Reading this book will convince you that even the way you breathe can make a difference.

As you will learn, the act of reading this book *is*, in itself, an initiation. But, contrary to Dante, whose patriarchal Christian Theology led him to warn his readers to "Abandon Hope, all ye who enter here," Barbara Ardinger, whose teachings embrace the matristic Goddess/Earth Mother Thealogy, might actually encourage her readers to: "Take Hope, all ye who enter here!"

For this is a book that certainly restores Hope, and one that will bring Light into your lives as well. Welcome to the Path of the Goddess, and Blessed Be!

Gloria Feman Orenstein
December 9, 1991

CONTENTS

Let Us Now Practice Her Presence

Once upon a time
ages and ages before the Garden of Eden was constructed
and had a landlord and walls and fiery angel guards —
Once upon a time
ages and ages before we fled to therapeutic couches
and became Adult Children Of —
Once upon a time
for ages and ages before time
we lived with our mothers and Our Mother.
Once upon a time
we planted and reaped and labored and danced together
we lived and lay down together in honor
and we were all the children of —
two-legged, and four-legged, and many-legged
winged and finned and rooted
crystalline and cloudy —
we were all Her children,
and the powers of the Power were present in our lives.
Once upon a time
She was present in our lives
every day and in every task
and everybody knew the Lady of the lands.
But now we stretch to find Her presence in the land
and we realize that Her time that once was
is coming round again
And once upon a time is nearly now.

INTRODUCTION:
LOOKING FOR AN EQUAL-
OPPORTUNITY RELIGION

A woman is sitting on a deep-green floor pillow in front of her altar. She's wearing comfortable clothing, perhaps her bathrobe, perhaps a favorite T-shirt and soft, roomy pants, and around her neck lies a string of cowrie shells she bought for $5 at a thrift store. The people she lives with know that this is her private time, so they're somewhere else, though the cats have, of course, strolled in to help with whatever's going on.

Music is playing (maybe Mozart, maybe Suzanne Ciani), and a vanilla potpourri is simmering nearby. On her altar (her mother's hope chest covered with scarves or a yard of paisley-print cotton from the remnant table) stand a carved wooden owl, a pack of Angel™ Cards scattered in a shallow dish, and a Christmas tree angel surrounded by a circle of round black stones.

The woman takes half a dozen deep, easy breaths, strokes the purring cat snuggled up beside her, and lights the two violet candles on the altar.

Most of us were introduced to religion in a church that looked pretty much like a courtroom. The spectators (us) were lined up in rows and it was expected that we would pay attention and be on our best behavior. Between the front row of spectators and the place where the important people stood was an empty space or even a low rail or a fence. The officers of this church/court were mostly men who stood between us and the holy place and talked to us like fathers addressing not-quite-well-behaved children. The judge was absent, though we all

1

knew he was an old man in a long robe, and the altar, which was on an elevated platform, always reminded us that he was both powerful and judgmental. *He knew* if we'd been good or bad.

There was no question about who was in charge.

Many of us are no longer satisfied with this setup. We want open access to the divine, and we've figured out that the divine essence of the world manifests as the world—in people, in plants and animals, in rivers and rocks. Many of us have read the books that explain how people used to worship a Mother Goddess who created the world and embodied the earth. We've read how people used to honor each other, how "thou shalt not kill" once really meant something. We've read some of the standard works, like *When God Was a Woman, The Civilization of the Goddess*, and *The Great Cosmic Mother*,[1] that describe the remains of the earliest religions, religions that were all but erased from existence by the later steppe- and desert-born religions. We've read what once was and wondered if it could be again.

Not only that, but we've also seen with our own eyes the condition of our planet, the polluted air and water, strip-mined and dumped-on land, overdevelopment at the expense of forests and plains. As more and more people begin to understand that the earth itself has value, we understand the value of an earth-based religion that teaches us to nourish and protect the earth and *all* of its inhabitants (even the ugly, unfriendly, and inanimate ones).

We've also begun to recognize the harm that imbalance between the sexes has wrought on all of us—on the violent men who have never learned any other way to be, on the abused and poverty-stricken women and children who remain at the bottom of the pecking order, on both men and women who want to explore their sensitive and intuitive natures but don't know how. If we're going to survive as individuals or as a planetary community, we need the Goddess and all Her gifts.

Intuitively, seriously, playfully, we've come to a new apprehension of what faith is about and we're creating an equal-opportunity religion. Based on images and figures found in caves and rubble and on hints found between the lines of the standard-brand holy books and dissertations, we're reinventing and re-creating the *genuine* old-time religion. We're building modern versions of the archaic religion of the Great Goddess, who was, and still is, the Queen of Heaven, Earth, and the Underworld.

When we can, we gather together to celebrate the eight festivals that mark the turning of the wheel of the year, the events that change our lives, and the phases of the moon that touch our lives.

Most of the time, however, we seem to be alone. We're not always sure we can reveal what we really believe, and we feel, deep down, that what people believe is a private matter. So when we attend to the Goddess, we do it alone or with a few close friends.

This book and its rituals were created to be used by a woman (or man) at her private altar in her personal space. These rituals are personal and unencumbered; that is, they don't require special equipment or elaborate scripts. They're personal, mystical poetry and visualization that touch the heart as well as the mind and help Everywoman practice the presence of the Goddess in her everyday life.

Some of these rituals can also be used by groups, staged with choral reading and dramatic costumes and props. You can use them as a point of inspiration to create additional poetry, beautiful altars, and wonderful music and movement.

What do you need to use this book? Not a lot, really. Here's a starter kit:

- Your active, fearless imagination
- An hour or two of quiet time in your living room or

bedroom, where you won't be disturbed by phone calls or
other mundane business

- A table, shelf, or chest to use as the foundation for your altar. (You can even bring the kitchen chopping block and
  lay it on the floor)
- Candles and holders, herbs, flowers, Goddess images (but
  only if you want to use them)
- Cherished objects to help you remember and to serve as
  props for your sacred drama (which is one definition of
  ritual)
- An intention or purpose
- Kindness and love for yourself and the Goddess's other
  children

Part I of this book focuses on thealogy.[2] We will explore
mystery, power, and cosmic issues. Since we are dealing with
mysteries, Chapters 1, 2, and 3 use paradox and extravagant
language to get at who this Goddess is that we worship in ritual.

Part II of this book sets forth the rules and tools of mystical, practical, poetical ritual. It's what I call "unencumbered ritual." We need to know how things have traditionally been
done, and we need to try out those things for ourselves to see
how they work and feel. But we also need to put ourselves into
our rituals, for rituals should not be recipes we follow without
thinking about what we're doing. We need to add and change
and move around until we're doing what feels right to us. We
need to be creative. The Goddess values humor and creativity,
and intention is more important than form.

Part III of this book takes us through a year in the path of
the Goddess. It's a year of rituals and celebrations devoted to
both light and dark. These ritual occasions are the phases of the
moon and the sun (the calendar year). Also called sabbats, the
eight yearly festivals keep us aware of the turning of the wheel

of the year, which is mirrored in the sky, on earth, and in the events of our lives.

The rituals are new ones, but they also contain echoes of old wisdoms and customs. Try them alone, try them with your friends, adapt them to your own times and circumstances. This book is intended only as a starting point. It can be your runway, but you have to fly on your own power. Consider my ideas. Try out the rituals I've written. But don't make this book your bible. Soar on your own power.

This is a personal book. Just for the record, it's the creation of a well-educated, middle-class WASP from Middle America. I hold a Ph.D. degree in English Renaissance literature with an emphasis on drama (Shakespeare) and I've been a teacher for a long time. I've also been a technical editor, and I'm a double Cancer whose Moon is in Gemini. That's what I am. Nevertheless, an individual's unique experiences reflect the whole and contain universal elements, so I know that my life experiences and yours share common ground.

This book is not all totally original thought, of course, and I happily acknowledge my debts to the ovular works in women's spirituality: Starhawk's *Truth or Dare*, Carol Christ's *Laughter of Aphrodite*, Riane Eisler's *Chalice and the Blade*, and several books by Z. Budapest, Barbara G. Walker, and Mary Daly.

Are men invited to participate in these women's rituals?

Yes, they are, but with the following consideration. For the past 5,000 or more years, men have tended to think they're entitled to be in charge. Men have tended to take over and women have tended to let them do it. This has been true even in so-called women's professions like nursing, in conferences for professional women, and, most obviously, in religion. Some women resent this takeover: things were going perfectly well until "they" came along and took charge. Some of us prefer to worship alone, therefore, or only with women until we've reclaimed our power and our creativity and the world is back in balance. (Some women believe balance will be a long time coming.) We do need leaders, of course, but leadership should be based on ability and knowledge, not on aggression and control.

So, dear brothers, if you can behave yourselves, please join our circles. Do the rituals yourselves, alone and in your own private spaces, and let yourselves feel the poetry. You're welcome in our circles when your presence and energy complement ours.

Let us all worship and work and play and dance the dance of life together. Let us all honor each other as beautiful, individual people and as best-beloved children of the Great Goddess.

Let's begin with a self-blessing, a blessing for our foremothers, and a blessing for our children. It is thus that time keeps turning.

A Self-Blessing

For this ritual, arrange to give yourself an uninterrupted hour in a room where you will not be disturbed. After your bath or shower, dress in your very most favorite clothes and jewelry (formal or casual or a combination of styles—something that makes you feel really good). Costume and adorn yourself so you look and feel like the *real you,* which is not necessarily the person seen by your business associates or anyone else in your public life.

Spend a few minutes gathering twelve things or representations of things (photographs or symbols) that you believe make an accurate picture of who you are. These things can include your daily organizer, the keys to your 1954 Edsel, a worn silver spoon your grandmother used in her kitchen, baby clothes from your ancestors or your children, or whatever you collect, your favorite childhood copy of *Swiss Family Robinson* or the paperback thriller you bought yesterday.

In addition, find a pink or bright spring green candle, a holder (preferably black, but it can be anything you like), and matches.

If you have a pet who wants to "help," invite it to help, but keep it away from the candle.

Sit in the middle of the floor and ask yourself, "Who am I? What makes me really Me?"

Now survey your collected things and begin to arrange them in a circle around you in this general order:

Behind you. Three things from your past or childhood. Things passed down to you. Things you've always loved.

Before you. Three things new to your life. Recent acquisitions, evidence of new interests. Things that indicate where you're going.

To your left. Three "left-brain" things. Things associated with words and numbers, logical thought, order, business, rational and intellectual thought.

To your right. Three "right-brain" things. Things associated with art, creativity, comfort and luxury, feelings, the religious or spiritual part of your life, beauty, and nature.

If you can, distribute these objects evenly throughout the four quarters in this circle of your life. If you can't, however, that's all right. Very few people are truly symmetrical. Put each thing in the quarter where it belongs, even if your circle ends up lop-sided.

Now light the pink or green candle and set it before you so it becomes the thirteenth element of the circle of your life.

Close your eyes, take several deep, easy breaths, and visualize or imagine the pink or green light from the candle surrounding you, filling your space, illuminating your life circle. Breathe in this light so it also fills your body. Feel the peace and love, the freshness and joy of this light in your life.

Feel the energy of the things around you rising and joining the candlelight. Feel this energy flowing into every cell in your body.

You can open your eyes and read the following blessing or

tape it beforehand and listen to it. You can also use it as a model to write your own words of blessing.

I bless myself
    and these things around me
    these things that make the circle of my life.
I bless myself
    and my past
For in blessing my past
    and these things that I bring from ages past
I become who I am now.
Good or bad, cheerful or painful, my past is a blessing,
    for it has formed me
    shaped me
    held me
    released me
    thrust me into the present.
I bless my past in me.

I bless myself
    and these things to my left and right.
I bless myself
    in my present
    the two halves of who I am today.
For in blessing both my intellect and my emotions
    and these things I gather into the life I live now
I recognize who I am now.
Left and right
    rational and spiritual
    words and images
    austerity and comfort—
I bring divisions together.
My present blesses me
    for it is how I am in the world

how I think and feel
how I act and live.
It pulls me out of the past
and thrusts me into the future.
I bless my life as it is today.

I bless myself
and the things that point to what is to come.
I bless myself
and my uncertainties, my potentialities, my future.
For in blessing what is new in my life
I move toward what I can be:
unknown but shown
unpredictable but mapped
potential to be fulfilled.
My future is waiting for me
more of who I am is waiting for me to be reborn.
I bless my life as it is now,
every day of my life.

Sit quietly for as long as you want to, feeling the energies of the things in the circle of your life. Contemplate who you have been, who you are now, who you are becoming. Realize that you are blessed in your life, that you are a blessing to other lives.

At the end, blow out the candle, put all your things into their proper places, and go on with your day.

A Blessing for Our Foremothers

For this ritual, first get out the old family photo albums and family souvenirs. Select photos of your mother, your aunts, your grandmothers, great aunts, great grandmothers, as many female ancestors as you can find. If you can't find photos, select artifacts—an antique silver spoon, a cameo broach, a crumpled ribbon, a hankie, a quilt. Lacking photos or objects, you can write their names on small pieces of white or lavender paper (parchment is best), and if you don't know their names, write titles like "father's great great grandmother." If your family doesn't save things, write something like "all my female relatives, living and dead" or "my foremothers, back to the beginning of time."

Line these photos or mementos up in front of you either on a table or simply on the floor and, for a few minutes, think about what they represent. Can you visualize this long line of female relatives? What are the countries of your origins? Where are these women? How far back does this line reach? What are these women doing? Visualize a web of women from all parts of the earth. This is most likely the best representation of your family tree.

Next, add to your collection photos of women you admire but are pretty sure you're not related to: Eleanor Roosevelt or Eleanor of Aquitaine, Cleopatra or Jinga Mbandi, Amelia Earhart or Marie Curie, Golda Meir or Indira Gandhi. Cut photos out of magazines or, if you don't want to mutilate a book or magazine, make a photocopy or hold the book open so that the photo you have chosen is visible.

Contemplate your collection of heras.[3] These are some of the women you will be blessing. You will also be attracting their powers to yourself.

Light two candles, lavender and red. Lavender is a traditional color of the Goddess and red is traditionally associated with the Mother aspect of the ancient Triple Goddess.

Lay your collection of photos and mementos in one or more circles (or a spiral) around the candles. Let the photos overlap; neatness doesn't count here, inclusiveness does.

Close your eyes and take a few deep, easy breaths. Visualize your mother, your grandmothers, aunts ... all the women of power in this long line encircling your candles. See yourself in your place in this line. Feel their power, their love, their labor, their successes. Feel their energy.

Sit quietly and think of the old family stories. Think about books you've read that have had active female protagonists, movies about women, myths of goddesses and heras. Remember the stories of strong, interesting women.

You can open your eyes and read the following blessing or tape it beforehand and listen to it. You can also use it as a model to write your own words of blessing.

> In the presence of the Most Holy Ones —
>> the Mothers of my body
>> the Grandmothers of my soul —
> I give thanks.
> I give thanks that I live
>> through their energy
>> through their love
>> through their labor.
>
> As a daughter/son of their wombs and works,
> I return their blessings:
>> I bless my mother/stepmother, [name].
>> I bless my grandmothers, [names].
>> I bless all the women of my family line,
>>> women whose names I know
>>> women whose names have been forgotten.
>> These women live still
>>> in and through all their daughters and sons.
> I bless the women of prehistory —
>> the strong, the unnamed, the forgotten.
> I bless the memories of the unknown women
>> who tamed fire
>> who created agriculture
>> who domesticated animals

    who invented crafts and sciences.
Their works have been forgotten
    or co-opted by men.
May we remember the true creators, our foremothers.

I bless the women of historical times,
    queens, warriors, judges, healers, witches —
    victims of exploitation
    victims of suppression
    victims of invading cultures.
Especially, I bless the Burned Ones,
    uppity women murdered during the Burning Times[4]
    tortured by a jealous Inquisition.
Never again.
Never again.
Never again will women be murdered.
I bless their souls
I bless their ashes.
Mothers and grandmothers, foremothers and foresisters —
    I, your descendant, bless your works.
    I, your child, bless your memory.
    I, your daughter/son, bless your blessing.

Look at your photos and other mementos again and contemplate your connections with all these women. Finally, extinguish your candles and go about your daily business.

A Blessing for Our Children

For this ritual, first find a photo of the earth taken from outer space, one of those famous photos of our beautiful blue planet. They've been published in many magazines, and stickers are also available, so it should be easy to find one. Place this photo on a table or on the floor between two white candles.

If you have children, grandchildren, nieces, or nephews, get photos of them (recent or old) and lay these photos in a circle around the picture of the earth.

Now find photos of other children, kids from all the countries of the world, all doing their kid things or assuming adult responsibilities. Make a circle with these photos around the two white candles, your own kids, and the earth.

Light your candles. Close your eyes and take several deep, easy breaths. Feel the blessing energy from the candles, the cleansing energy of the white light. Feel the energy of all these children, both at their most raucous and adventuresome play, and in repose, study, or sleep.

Spend some time thinking about the energy and wonder children bring to our lives — seeing ordinary things through their new eyes, for example, or living each day as a new adventure. Think about what children bring to the world, what their potential can bring to the world. Think about the state of the world: progressive and repressive politics, famine and hunger, wars and threats of war, the "childization" of poverty. Think about the state of the planet: polluted air and water, burning forests, suffering and dying birds, animals, and people. Is this the kind of place you want your kids and their kids to live in?

Read the following blessing or tape it beforehand and listen to it or use it as a model to make up your own words.

Children of the living earth —
    I bless you.
Children of so many living cultures —
    I bless your ways.
Children of our hopes and lives —
    I bless your wishes.

I bless your games, your work, your learning,

I bless your dreams, your ambitions, your reaching for-
    ward.

But our earth is imperfect—
        our land is wounded,
        our air and water are wounded,
        our children are wounded.
But people are at war—
        nation against nation,
        tribe against tribe,
        our children are wounded.
Children of genocide,
        I bless you.
        May you flourish.
Children of poverty,
        I bless you.
        May you always have enough to eat and drink.
Children of heedless development,
        I bless you.
        May you live in peace.
Children of our wounded, stumbling planet,
        I bless you.
And I promise you:
        I will act to ensure you a future
        I will act to restore your home.
Bright blessings.

PART ONE

PRACTICING THE PRESENCE OF THE GODDESS

PRACTICING
THE PRESENCE
OF THE GODDESS

The most, and the least, that we can say about the Goddess is that *She Is*. Like Jehovah and Popeye, *She Is What She Is*. She Is All That Is, She always was, She is now, and She always will be.

That's it. But these concepts are high and mighty, and they're also pretty high-fallutin'. In this section, we'll bring them down to earth. We'll ground philosophy in the material, in its matter.

The way to get all this philosophy grounded is to practice the presence of the Goddess. As we live each day on earth, we become more aware each day of the ways She is present in our lives.

I'm not alone in these thoughts and feelings, and neither are you. We stand in the company of millions of people, some living in the here and now, some living in Persephone's realm of the dead or in the land of Grandmother Hel. We're part of generations and cultures all around the world, all the people who have found the feminine principle in nature, in themselves, even hiding in the hearts of the standard-brand religions.

Some of these people have been called mystics. If you wonder about mystics, read any chapter of Matthew Fox's *Original Blessing*, which is a book about mystics throughout history, about some of the people who see the divine in everything they look at, who perceive the blessing of life and the world.

1

AN M-WORD, TWO W-WORDS, AND AN R-WORD

In a world apparently ruled by technology and testosterone, people go to church or temple maybe once a week, usually less. In this world, our daily life is concerned with what's on the six o'clock news or what's happening at the mall. We turn to our gods only when we need a favor.

There have always been people, however, who are just a little bit different from the rest of us. They're the rare ones who take seriously the idea of the divine manifesting daily in the world. They take seriously the idea that we should cherish others as we cherish ourselves and that we should also cherish ourselves at least as much as we cherish the things we buy. They actually feel a mind-fixing connection with both heaven and earth. They also see and hear things the rest of us don't.

So we call them crazy or weird. Or maybe we refer to them as saints or poets or artists. Occasionally we even throw the M-word at them: These foolish people are mystics.

Mysticism

Now mysticism does not necessarily have to be what the standard-brand religions have been telling us it is. It does not have to mean running away from the world, the flesh, and the devil, and retreating into a cloister or a mountaintop cave. It's not hysteria, it's not escapism, it doesn't require any special equipment or qualifications.

Mysticism is not a matter of doing anything special; it's a way of life. It's recognizing that we're related to everyone else, even those who don't look like us or talk like us. It's recognizing the living fact that everyone on earth is a child of Mother Earth and that eagles and eels and beetles and green leaves are all Her children too. It's really acting out the Golden Rule and seeing the star stuff of which we're all made.

Mysticism in the tradition of the Goddess is living an ordinary life, not acting spacy or sanctimonious or as if we were specially "chosen." It's making a living, making car payments, disciplining our kids. It's doing regular things but doing them in an attitude that some call mindfulness. This means being aware of what we're doing, reflecting on our thoughts. It's living with raised consciousness.

As I see it, then, mysticism is purely practical, and it helps us get along in the world. It could help everyone get along by getting things done efficiently and gracefully. It's bringing high concepts down to earth, grounding lofty ideals like "ethical behavior," "lawfulness," and "right living."

Mystics help it all hang together. They patch the rips in the web of life and give limbo lessons to people who keep tripping up in the dance of life.

You may not think you're a mystic, or maybe you've just never thought of religion in this way. You might be surprised. Do an inventory of your own path of faith. If you're anything

like me, you've come to your present belief along a
path. I was born into a Calvinist church and explored most of
the nooks and crannies of New Thought, metaphysics, and
Eastern religions before I got where I am now.

When you've completed your own inventory, try the following ritual. (I like to do it under the full moon.)

A Ritual for the Path of My Faith

If you have any physical souvenirs (like your christening gown
or Sunday school attendance pins or Unitarian Universalist Association card), gather them and lay them in chronological order
in a wide zig-zag (snake track) in front of you. If all you've kept
are the memories, write names or vignettes on paper or cards
and lay them on the floor. If you have memories or fantasies
from former lives, add them to the path. Finally, get something
that symbolizes what you believe now and hold it in both hands.
This could be a pine cone, a favorite crystal, a feather, or a Goddess image. It could also be a handful of "empty" space that only
appears to be empty, for it is really full of consciousness.

Sit comfortably, facing your past and holding your present,
and read the following words or tape them beforehand and listen to them or use them as a model to make up your own words.

I face the path of my faith.
This is the way I've come,
    the journey my soul has taken
    to bring me where I am today.
I recall the people I've met on this path,
    teachers all,
    kind and unkind —
Whatever they did, they walked with me awhile
and showed me their paths.
I bless their being and their teaching.

I remember events and encounters along the way,
> pleasant or painful,
> > always instructive —
Whatever happened, it was useful,
and in its own integrity it was beautiful.
I learned to follow my own path,
I learned where I must go,
I bless the path of my past.

Still holding the symbol of your present, turn around. Turn your back on your past, put it behind you.

> Holding my present in my own hands,
> I face my future now.
> I face a new path every morning,
> > every day I step forward on an unknown path,
> > a unique path sprinkled with the star stuff
> > of the Goddess.
> In Her presence, past, present, and future are one time
> and I'm where I'm supposed to be —
> now and always:
> > my path is in Her.

Close your eyes and think about what this means to you. If you want to, begin writing a mystical journal.

Worship and Witches

The M-word leads our thoughts to the first W-word: as we live in our everyday lives, we find ourselves engaging more and more in *worship*. Before it becomes action, worship is focus; it is what is called mindfulness. To some people worship means keeping an "attitude of gratitude," to others worship is seeing the "worth-ship" in life. Let's consider what worship means to us.

It used to be kneeling down and raising the eyes to the ethereal skies and saying, "I obey." It used to be following strict procedures, sticking to an order of service. Deviation used to be swiftly punished.

Today, however, especially among mystics, worship is saying, "I respect." It's creating altars and making music. It's saying, "I love and cherish because I recognize something of which I'm a part. I want to celebrate my recognition."

You can worship in a specifically defined holy place or you can worship just about anywhere on our planet, which is itself a holy place. You can sit or stand near your own altar and see how that altar embodies the earth and all the earthly, earthy powers. You can worship with silent prayer, do a private ritual in your bedroom first thing in the morning, or gather and hold hands with like-minded and like-hearted people to strengthen your connections with one another and with all our kin on earth.

Worship doesn't require any special equipment or qualifications. To a mystic, worship is, in fact, a way of life. We just seem to do it all the time, whether we're paying much attention to it or not.

Although all the standard-brand religions, both Western and Eastern, have produced their own mystics and their own kinds of worship, some of us who accept our own mysticism and worship in unorthodox ways use the second W-word to describe ourselves: we're Witches.

Who is a Witch? If we took a survey, we could probably find as many definitions of the word as there are people who use it. Twenty years ago, for example, we were told to say "I am a Witch" three times and really think about what we were saying. We thought that made us a Witch.

Why use the word "Witch"? It seems to be a scary word, with all its connotations of green skin and spells and evil decrepitude. A less threatening word is "Wicca," which is said to come from Middle English words that mean "wise" and "to bend." A Witch, or Wiccan, is thus a wise person who bends power.

The words Witch and Wiccan are not, however, strictly synonymous. Many people believe that "Witch" refers specifically to spiritual feminists (well, OK, an occasional man, too) whose worship is focused on the Goddess, whereas "'Wiccans" are both men and women who worship both the old gods and the goddesses. It's also pretty safe to say that those who call themselves Wiccans generally tend to be closer to ceremonial magic in their rituals than most who call themselves Witches are, Witches being famously eclectic. But these distinctions are not universal. I know several male Witches (male Witches are never called warlocks or wizards) who are as devoted to the Goddess as I am, and many people who prefer "Wicca" simply because it sounds more respectable.

Like some other Witchy authors, I prefer the blunter word, "Witch." It gets people's attention. Because I am a kind, intelligent person, I can demonstrate to the world that "wicked" does not automatically define "Witch." By saying I'm a Witch, I can help restore honor to the thousands or millions of alleged witches who were burned by the Christian Inquisition during the European Renaissance. By saying I'm a Witch, I'm telling you what my religion is.

A Witch accepts the reality of the Great Goddess who was worshipped 30,000 or more years ago and whose followers were persecuted by the fathers (the infamous patriarchs) of the desert churches.

Today, most people who call themselves Witches worship the Goddess. Many Witches also worship Her son/consort, the Horned God. Modern Witches, who are included in a diverse group called Neo-Pagans,[5] follow an ancient, earth-based religion whose focus is on a Mother down here with us instead of a Father way up there, far away from us.

We Witches are reviving ancient ways of worshipping. We're reinventing the archaic, earthy mysticism that says the flesh is holy and the spirit is just finely strained matter (or, conversely, matter is just clotted, lumpy spirit).

Since we don't know, however, exactly how people living as far back as the Stone Age worshipped the Goddess, we who live today have to use our best guesses about the ancient forms of worship. We use our intuition, our vision, and hints and suggestions from many sources, including archaeological discoveries and evidence from books in which the old ways were described in order to anathematize them.

This makes us a very eclectic bunch, and when we worship we often make it up as we go along. Our worship is ordered, but it's seldom orderly. That's one reason why there are so many traditions and processes, so many ways of doing rituals (which all seem to work), and so many books that seem to contradict each other. I believe that they really complement each other. I believe that Witchcraft is catholic in the original sense of the word: general and all-inclusive.

Ritual

When Witches worship, how do we do it? The answer to this question lies in the R-word: we use rituals.

Most simply, a ritual is a repeatable, and often repeated, action that has a specific meaning and an objective or intention. The actions and the words, or both, serve to put the person doing the ritual into an altered state of consciousness, which may be worshipful or experimental or playful. The altered state of consciousness gets us in touch with invisible powers, which may be intrinsic (our untapped imagination and unfertilized creativity) or extrinsic (goddesses, elemental spirits, devas, etc.), and we then work with these powers. Ritual is both a process and a procedure. The steps common to most rituals will be discussed in Chapter 4.

In its secular sense of "habitual action," a ritual can be your customary morning routine. It's the foggy, groggy, automatic way you get out of bed, go to the bathroom, wash, and get dressed. Your morning ritual can include all the little informal ceremonies you create to bless your day and make it work better. It can be the way you get ready to do some task.

Ritual elements in our daily lives can be mundane (the way we put our socks on) but we can also use rituals to make our lives more beautiful, like setting fresh flowers on the table or desk, unpacking and washing Grandma's dishes for Thanksgiving, writing thank-you notes, or helping our children prepare for their first day of school or graduation (major rituals in themselves).

In this sense of enlivening our days and making them graceful and memorable, ritual enhances our lives. The repeatability and predictability of ritual add a bit of security to our ages of chaos. Doing a ritual puts us into the right mood. Ritual can bring us comfort or inspiration. It can link us to the past and help us prepare for the future by making today more meaningful. That was the purpose of the little ritual you did earlier in this chapter.

Carried to extremes, of course, even the grandest ritual can also dig us more deeply into our ruts, and that's why we need to remember the sacred sense of ritual. Instead of ruts, rituals can create paths.

Did you learn to close your eyes and fold your hands when you pray, and do you still do so? That's one ritualistic element of worship. So is the order of service at a church or temple. You always know pretty much what is going to happen and when, whether you're attending High Holy Mass, a Pentecostal revival, or a Bar Mitzvah. In almost any given worship service, the ritual is written out.

Some pagan rituals are simple and quiet, like the act of selecting beautiful, meaningful objects for your altar and arranging them on it. Lighting a candle, focusing your attention, and
speaking or reading a dramatic verse is a simple, private ritual.
At the other extreme is an outdoor spiral dance for 500 people,
accompanied by a pagan dance band of doumbeks, frame
drums, rattles, and tambourines. The spiral dance winds along
its own labyrinthine path around a central point (altar or bon-
fire), faster and faster and faster. It stirs up enormous energy
and is something we should all experience at least once in our
lives, even if we end up in breathless collapse.

In between the two extremes are private or public rituals to
celebrate the full and new moons, to empower a special project
(as I did when I started to work in earnest on this book), to
beckon love or money into our lives, to celebrate a friend's good
fortune, to bless a new home. Any occasion is an occasion for
ritual, alone or with friends.

2

THE PRACTICE OF THE
PRESENCE OF THE GODDESS

As our Mother Earth and all her children dance in the Age of Aquarius (or the New Age or the Millennium), more and more people are wondering if the things we measure only with our minds and machines are enough to nourish our lives. We're asking if the things we buy and sell are what we really want, after all. We're looking for the invisible, nourishing dimension of life that hasn't been really accessible since the Industrial Revolution lined us all up and started whirring, cranking, and belching at us. We've been reaching forward to new and improved technology or backwards to the so-called "traditional" values. But I wonder ... have we been reaching in the right direction?

What would happen if we reached *inward* instead? What if we laid hands on the small, dark, precious seeds of creativity and love that rest deep inside us all? Instead of focusing on outward things to help and heal us, what would happen if we focused inward?

What would happen if we began to practice the presence of the Goddess?

Re-creating the Mystical Dimension

What I'm talking about, of course, is something men and women have been doing for millennia: re-creating the mystical dimension in their lives, in life itself. We are renewing our personal mystical connection to the divine.

What I'm also talking about is a significant change in mystical practice—not a forswearing of earthly life and material goodies and a retreat to a mountaintop, but a thoughtful, heartfelt return to the much-maligned earth plane.

As far as we can tell from the archaeological evidence, the archaic, rural followers of the Old Religions lived closer to the earth than we do today. They called her Mama and lived in harmony with the light and the dark, observing and celebrating the phases of the moon and the year. Their modern children—we who call ourselves Neo-Pagans or Witches or other followers of the new earth-based religions—are returning to or reinventing these ancient observations and celebrations.

Author/astrologer Demetra George says that one reason we're re-creating our new/old religion is that the Goddess Herself is re-emerging into the world. Like the moon, Her life moves in phases and cycles. Her new moon phase was the dawn of the Upper Paleolithic (ca. 38,000 B.C.E.), when humankind walked out of Africa and began to settle in western Europe. Her waxing phase, says George, began about 11,000 B.C.E., when women discovered agriculture and invented cooking. This phase lasted through the Neolithic, and we have much evidence of worship of the feminine principle, the unnamed Great Goddess, in ruins throughout Old Europe (beginning ca. 7,000 B.C.E.) and in the earliest cities, such as Jericho (9,500 B.C.E.),

Catal Huyuk (6,500 B.C.E.), and Halicar (5,600 B.C.E.). The Goddess's waning phase began about 3,000 B.C.E. with the rise of the earliest patriarchal religions. She has been sleeping in Her natural dark moon phase for 5,000 years and is now awakening to begin Her next new moon phase.

We're observing and celebrating the re-emergence of open worship of the Goddess after a thousand years of hidden, underground worship. To use the current jargon, we're changing our paradigms, seeing new patterns and influences in old lives. We're merging the sacred with the secular. We're recalling our true essence, which is both immanent and transcendant. We're reaching into mysticism and juggling with it. We're engaged in life both as it is and as it can be.

Does this sound paradoxical? It is. It's difficult, in fact, to write about mysticism because words are intrinsically inadequate to the job. In writing this book, I'm using a left-brain medium to approach a right-brain process, and what comes out are paradox and extravagant language. You'll also find paradox and extravagant language in books on Zen and yoga, in books on the Sufi and Hassidic ways, in the words of the Christian and New Thought mystics, and in the Course in Miracles books.

I think this fact helps to explain why most of the books on Goddess ritual are like cookbooks: it's easier to give a recipe than to wander around in the batter. How do we describe the indescribable? How do we visualize the unseeable, apprehend the unknowable, ponder the unthinkable?

As simply as I can say it, mysticism—the practice of the presence of the Goddess—is a way to get centered in your own center. Other people have other names for this center: God, Christ Consciousness, Higher Self, Nirvana, Unity With All, Reverence For Life. I call this center *Goddess* and *Inner Self,* "inner" because I don't like the hierarchical implications of "higher" self.

Of the many paths to this center, I believe that the following four are the most familiar and the most relevant to practicing the presence of the Goddess.

Deep Thought. The first path is largely intellectual. We need intellectual content—facts, history, theory, philosophy—and intelligent discussion of that content so we don't fall into silliness or rote repetition of practices handed down from some god or guru. We need to think for ourselves. We need to think about what we're doing, not do it just because someone said we should. When you adopt a mystical sensibility, therefore, do not abandon your common sense; keep some healthy skepticism in the mix.

Good Works. The second path is more active. We're not all Mother Teresa or Albert Schweitzer, to be sure, but we can do good works. We can do them out of kindness and the recognition that we're all related, and not out of fear that we won't go to heaven if we don't. We can do little things and big deals, be polite to someone or give a large donation to charity. Even our smallest good works are beneficial. They're not only mutually beneficial, but they also add that much more kindness to the aura of the planet.

Experiential Play. The third path is both active and intellectual. This is the scientific path (maybe it's technological as well), and ritual may be its most obvious application. An experientially-oriented person does enough research to create a ritual with the correct associations and actions, does the ritual according to a written or unwritten agenda, and makes notes on performance and outcome. On this experiential path tread ceremonial magicians and other people who manipulate realities to get results. Because these are such highly serious people most of the time, I call the path Experiential *Play* to remind us all to take it seriously without becoming too solemn. Mistakes and laughter are a valuable part of the process.

Devotion. The fourth path, like deep thought, can be passive and, like anything else, devotion can be taken to extremes. I see it as pure love, as an unconditional love that sees clearly and focuses on the center. Devotion needs to stay grounded, though, and sometimes it needs to be tough. It always requires a good dose of common sense.

As the rest of this book will show, when we practice the presence of the Goddess we follow all four of these paths at once. Sometimes we emphasize one path or another, but the ideal is to keep in balance. That is, we need to add feeling to our thought and think about what we're feeling. We need to be kind and also brave enough to try new things.

This is what I mean by mindfulness. It is simply keeping your mind focused on something. Traditional mindfulness has meant focusing on a mantra, a yantra (visual symbol), or a chant or affirmation. I have a friend, for example, who once spent several months setting the alarm on her wristwatch to go off every five minutes. Every time the alarm sounded, she said a brief prayer for her personal health and the health of the planet. That's mindfulness.

I want to enlarge this process: let's turn it into "remember-fulness" and get rid of the alarm. How? Try this. Go about your regular day at the office or the plant or at home, and do all the zillions of things you normally do. At the same time, reserve one small, side corner of your mind to remember. Anytime you come to a stopping place, pull the contents of this small, side corner forward and remember. Remember who you are—a divine child, part of the consciousness of the planet, a member of a community. Remember where you are—sheltered by the flowing blue cloak of our Mother, living on the skin of an organism named Earth, living as a child of the oldest goddess, who is older than names.

With a split-second wordless thought or with a full-blown

ritual, practice the presence of the Goddess as you live your everyday life.

One of the best books about mindfulness could be a Zen text, but it's really one of the best of the Christian mystical books: *The Practice of the Presence of God*. This book contains the thoughts of Brother Lawrence, a humble monk who to this day is much loved and admired because he practiced the presence of his god all the time. He engaged in mindfulness while he was scrubbing the floors, doing laundry, or cleaning the kitchen. Because he eschewed the glamour of psychic phenomena to follow a path of pure devotion, Brother Lawrence seems to be a Zen monk, or perhaps a Bodhisattva or a practitioner of bhakti yoga. He didn't argue or preach (although he did write spiritual letters), and he didn't do anything spectacular. He just walked around in his life practicing the presence of his god, and that practice still spreads joy to all who encounter him, if only through his book.

Try it yourself. Don't talk about what you believe to people who really aren't interested. Don't show off what you can do because you believe in something. Just walk around in your life remembering who you are and who She is.

In our own ways, then, we can all follow the example of Brother Lawrence. Let's keep the Goddess in mind. Let's take Her to work with us and remember to work as effectively and creatively as we can. Let's take Her shopping with us and buy healthful food and items with biodegradable or recyclable packaging, and—as long as people are hungry or homeless—let's try not to buy so many luxury goodies. Let's remember that She's everybody's mother when we're stuck in traffic or in an all-hands meeting called by the boss for 4:45 P.M. on a Friday. Let's even keep Her at home with us.

A Ritual of Rememberfulness

Bring to your personal space something you use or keep with you during the day—your daily organizer, a floppy disk, your car keys. Hold this object, which is your memory aid, in both hands and read the following words or tape them beforehand and listen to them or use them as a model to make up your own words.

Hold your memory aid up to your forehead, holding it in both hands.

> I remember.
> Every day, I remember,
> and I think about who I am—
>   my role in my family
>   the work I do
>   how I play.
> I think about where I am
> I think about
>   what I do with my time
>   what I do with my money
>   what I do with my energy.
> While I'm busy doing,
> some small, secret corner of my mind
> reminds me
>   that I am Her child
>   that we are all related
>   that I can add kindness to the aura of the planet.

Think about these words for a few minutes. Think without evaluation, and if your thoughts wander, follow them. When you're ready, move your memory aid to your stomach and hold it there in both hands.

I remember and feel.
Every day, I remember and feel.
I have strong feelings about my life
    about my family and friends
    about my work
    about the world.
And I remember that these feelings are valid
and I honor them.
My feelings influence my thinking and my acting
and I remember to temper my thoughts and actions.
So while I'm busy thinking and doing,
    I remember to feel
    I remember that I feel
    I remember how I feel.
I remember how I feel when I remember
    that I am Her child
    that we are all related
    that I can add kindness to the aura of the planet.

Ponder the feelings these words elicit in you for a few minutes.
If your thoughts wander, follow them. When you're ready, move
your memory aid to your heart and hold it there in both hands.

I remember and love.
Every day, I remember and love.
I love and honor
    the people in my life
    the work I do
    the way I look
    the things I own.
I remember and love with clear sight
    with understanding
    without illusions

> with an open heart.
> While I'm busy thinking and doing and feeling,
> I remember that love embraces and shelters all things.
> And I remember to act on my love, remembering
>> that I am Her child
>> that we are all related
>> that I can add kindness to the aura of the planet.

Consider these words for a while, think about your past experiences, times you have loved wisely and times you have loved foolishly. If your thoughts wander, follow them. When you're ready, smile and go on about your day. Whenever you encounter your memory aid during the day, remember to remember.

There are many ways to practice the presence of the Goddess in our everyday lives. Here are a few.

Listen to music. Numerous tapes of Goddess music are available in metaphysical stores, mainstream record stores (usually in the New Age music section), in catalogs like Ladyslipper,[6] and at New Age, Renaissance, Whole Earth, and Womanspirit fairs.

Cure your addiction to the news, which focuses on crisis after crisis, and inane talk-radio by listening to Goddess music in your car. Start and end your day with it. I'm convinced it's better for your mental state than listening to the news, though I am certainly not suggesting that you give up knowing what's going on in the world. What I'm suggesting is *balance.*

Look at art.[7] Find art that honors women and art by women — paintings, prints, posters, sculpture, fiber art, found art, calendars, etc. An especially eloquent book is *The Power of Feminist Art.* As you look at a piece of art, consider the courage of the woman who made it, think about what the art means (especially if it's feminist art, which can be beautiful and scary at the same time), and examine your own resonance with this art.

Appreciate your friends, former friends, relations, and pets. We're all created in *Her* image. The Goddess myths, eons older than the Genesis myth, describe how She gave birth to the universe and everything in it. (Well, as one who lives with two cats, I do not hold Her responsible for fleas.) In 1987, geneticists presented evidence that we are all descended from an African "mitochondrial Eve."[8] If that is so, her DNA lives in everyone alive today, and it means we really are all related.

Consider the love and support your exchange with your friends, the help and information you exchange with both co-workers and people you hardly know, the unconditional love and entertainment you receive from the animals that live with you. Consider the lessons you've learned from the people who are no longer in your life, and *why* they're no longer in your life. Practice that good old "attitude of gratitude."

Read good books. As a visit to your local bookstore will show, there's a whole library of Goddess books already on the shelves and more on the way. Some are listed in the Bibliography for this book.

But don't just read passively. React to what you're reading. Talk back to the author, either in your mind, by writing notes in the margin (if you own the book), or by writing letters to the author. Synthesize what you learn in one book with what you learn in other books so you have a rounded vision and relatively bias-free information.

Wear Goddess jewelry. If you work or hang out where wearing a yoni or a labrys or a pentacle would be troublesome, try a simple crescent moon, a silver flower, or a ring with a meaningful semiprecious stone in it, like moonstone, tourmaline, or turquoise. Keep in mind that you're not wearing this jewelry to advertise but to help you remember. If you prefer to do so, wear your jewelry under your clothes. I wear the word YES on a gold chain and seldom wear it outside because it's a message to me, not to the world at large.

Take action. Recycle (of course) and reduce your conspic-
uous consumption. Smile at other drivers on the highway and
say thank you to servers and busboys and clerks.

If you feel strongly about something, do something about it.
Take political action. You can write letters to the President or
participate in Amnesty International's "urgent action" projects,
which involve writing a letter on behalf of a prisoner of conscience.[9] You can join a local organization or a national one.
You can do volunteer work or take part in a demonstration for
your cause.

Redecorate your space. Put a fresh flower, a potted plant,
a pretty shell, or a feather on your desk at work. Hang symbols
of elemental fire, water, air, and earth on the walls at home. Set
a candle in a beautiful holder and a goblet on a doily with a
photo of your grandmother or a tarot card. Install a Goddess
image—anyone from Isis or Athena to Miss Piggy or Barbie—
in a place of honor in your home. Set up an altar (see Chapter
5), and redecorate it for each major festival. Decorate your
home as much as you can get away with.

Put a bumpersticker on your car or on a wall. What the
bumpersticker says, of course, may be dictated by where you
live. LOVE YOUR MOTHER is fairly inoffensive, whereas WIZ-
ARDS HAVE CRYSTAL BALLS AND HALLOW WIENIES
might get you more attention than you really want. My bumpersticker says THE GODDESS IS ALIVE AND MAGIC IS
AFOOT. I used to have one that said TRUST GOD—SHE PRO-
VIDES; it got vandalized (several times). Now I have one above
my bedroom door that says WHERE THERE'S A WITCH
THERE'S A WAY and one above my computer that says
WITCHES CAN SPELL.

Take classes in women's spirituality. You can learn mask
and rattle construction, drumming or belly dancing, beginning
Wicca, herbalism and aromatherapy, jewelry making, weaving,

creative writing, and divination (tarot, I Ching, runes, etc.) or other psychic sciences. Before you sign up, however, ascertain the orientation of the teacher. You might not enjoy spending time with a patriarchal astrologer or a musician who insists that drumming was invented by and for men.

Get on the good mailing lists so you find out when Z. Budapest, Starhawk, Vicki Noble, Diane Stein, and others are going to be doing workshops in your area.[10]

Create your own art. Because it alters your consciousness and is repetitive, the act of creation is itself ritualistic. The very essence of the Goddess is creation, and nothing She created is junk. Since we're all created in Her image or, as some believe, we're literally part of Her body because we're living creatures, everything we create is beautiful and precious, if only to our Mother. So don't worry—you're not competing with Van Gogh, you don't have to be frustrated because you're not a "real artist," and you don't even have to show anyone what you make. (If you want to draw, but don't believe you can, *Drawing on the Right Side of the Brain*, by Betty Edwards can be very helpful.)

Multi-media art, or found art, can be more expressive than drawing or painting because it helps you see things in new ways. Found art means combining things you find—rocks you pick up, feathers, twigs and other pieces of trees and bushes, dried flowers and herbs, shells, the wishbone from your baked chicken. You can add ribbons, glitter, T-shirt paint (the kind that comes in squeeze bottles), beads of all kinds, fortune cookie fortunes, and orphan earrings. You don't need formal training or expensive tools. You can use white glue and string to hold things together, and your symbols can be traditional ones or personal ones that you thought up yourself.

Here's how to make your art-making a ritual. Create a tidy place on the floor or a table, gather all your goodies around you, listen to your favorite tape (or a new one), and close your eyes. Welcome designs into your mind, either things you've seen in "real life" or new visions. When you open your eyes, let your creative mind travel into your hands and just begin to idly manipulate your found objects until something clicks. You might also have something specific in mind, like the creation of a new altar tool or a small symbol to hang on your rearview mirror. You can do something as simple as tying multi-colored ribbons around the stem of a goblet or a project as complex as a wall-size collage of postcards, feathers, seed pods, and pieces of jewelry. Let yourself play. I once combined an upright spark plug, two white marbles, and some dried rosebuds on a maroon scallop shell to make a nifty little god.

It's said that fairies love ribbons. If you want to attract the Old Ones, or just hang something pretty in your room, get a smallish embroidery hoop and enough yard-long pieces of ribbon to go around the hoop and glue one end of each piece of ribbon to the hoop. (It comes out looking like a windsock.) Use thread or more ribbon to make a hanger for the hoop. You can also add beads, bells, and feathers, and then hang it by a window to catch a breeze.

One warning. My son quoted this to me the other night: "A work of art is never finished; it is simply abandoned."

As you're putting your art together, be rememberful. What does this feather or twig remind you of? The joy of flight and the power of an acorn? Why are you using these colors of beads or ribbon or yarn? What feelings do these colors arouse in you? Are you working (playing) with curves or straight lines? Why? How does this whole process feel to you? How does this ritual of creation alter your consciousness, and what are you going to do with your altered consciousness?

As you are beginning your project, or when you've completed your work and step back to admire it, read these words or tape them beforehand and listen to them or use them as a model to make up your own words.

As She created from Herself
    a work of art
    and called it the universe,
So do I create from the things I find
    my own work of art
    and call it remembrance.
As She provided all these treasures
    for our nourishment and pleasure,
So do I accept the things I find
    and use them to create new worlds.
As She labored and played,
So do I play and remember Her.

Talk to yourself, sing to yourself. We all do it all the time anyway. We're programming our minds to be either user-hostile or user-friendly. We're creating our own consciousness, and what we create in our own consciousness we also create in the consciousness of the planet. Wouldn't it be better for all of us if we spent all that self-talk re-creating the presence of the Goddess?

Self-talk has other names: mindfulness, silent prayer, awareness, meditation, affirmatory repetition. But it doesn't matter what you call it, so long as you just do it.

You can choose a mantra: OM. MAMA. AMEN. Sounded vocally or subvocally, a mantra sets up vibrations and resonances that create all kinds of wonderful effects in your mind and body.

If you don't want a traditional mantra, select a Goddess name and do a few minutes of research to find out what Her attributes and associations are. Then, keeping what you've learned in mind, sound Her name: SAULE. ISIS. BRIGIT. AMATERASU. Sound slowly, drawing out all vowel sounds, extending the consonant sounds as much as possible as well. KAAAAALLLLLIIIII. Sound the name as long as your breath lasts (and as you do this sounding, your breath capacity will grow) and let the sounds swirl around your throat, ears, and heart. Do it aloud in your car in traffic (you might even create a "found" traffic goddess: DRIVESAFELY). Sound your Goddess name every morning in the shower, as loud as you want to, and sound it under your breath whenever you're doing anything that doesn't require complete, left-brain attention. (That is, sound the name of Juno Habundia before and after you balance your checkbook, but not during.)

When you're ready, move from self-talk and sounding Goddess names to singing or chanting. There are dozens of chants on audio tape,[11] some very simple and easy to learn, some more complex. Here are some of my favorites.

Begin with Deena Metzger's wonderful Goddess Chant: ISIS, ASTARTE, DIANA, HECATE, DEMETER, KALI, INANNA. Two, very different, versions of this chant can be found on Charlie Murphy's album "Catch the Fire" and on "From the Goddess," performed by Robert Gass and On Wings of Song.[12] Listen to both of these, and while your goosebumps are still blooming, learn the chant yourself. You can also use other names to pull other associations into your consciousness. BRIGIT, ATHENA, ARTEMIS, CERRIDWEN, GREEN TARA, MAWU, YAMAYA. Teach your chants to your friends and sing them in unison, in parts, or as rounds.

Here are a few more Goddess chants.

By Buffy Ste. Marie: THE GODDESS IS ALIVE AND MAGIC IS AFOOT.

By Starhawk: SHE CHANGES EVERYTHING SHE TOUCHES, AND EVERYTHING SHE TOUCHES, CHANGES.

Based on a chant, "We all come from the God," by Richard Quinn and also attributed to Z. Budapest: WE ALL COME

FROM THE GODDESS,/AND TO HER WE SHALL RE-
TURN,/LIKE A DROP OF RAIN,/FLOWING TO THE OCEAN.

Another mantra that runs through my mind whenever I
shift into neutral invokes the Tibetan goddess Green Tara: OM
TARE TUTARE TURE SOHA. When we repeat this mantra,
we're asking this Goddess, who is also called She Who Leads
Across, to protect us from both our existential fears and
chronic diseases.

One of my favorite Goddess songs was printed in the Great
Goddess issue of *Heresies*.[13] It's sung to the familiar tune, "Jesus
Loves Me."

> Isis loves me, this I know
> Mother God has told me so.
> She is strong and so are we
> Fighting for equality.
> Yes, Isis loves me
> Yes, Isis loves me
> Yes, Isis loves me
> Our Lady told me so.

Add new verses with other two-syllable Goddess names:

MAWU
KALI
BRIGIT
IX CHEL   } loves me, this I know ...
NIKE
JUNO
VENUS

3

APPROACHING
THE GODDESS

No matter what we worship—money, MTV, the Mississippi River—we need to understand what we're worshipping. We need to understand what the power is and how we respond to it. We need to be clear about the transaction of worship, how the energy is exchanged.

What kinds of energies are we invoking in ourselves when we do a ritual? What is the source of those energies? What other kinds of energies are invoked? When we create and enact a ritual, whether it's a simple meditation or a complex dramatic reenactment of a myth—what is the return on our investment of thought, work, experience, and devotion? What is the new frame of mind our ritual takes us to?

When it's the Goddess we're worshipping, these questions are particularly important, for we're dreaming up an ancient deity, reinventing a religion, re-creating a way of life. She's not a fad, She's not Jehovah in drag, She's not a marble cliché, She's not pretty flowers on a sunny day, She's not our fairy godmother, She's not our local, self-designated high priestess. But, yes, to some people She indubitably is all these things. The

Goddess is at least as complex as the aggregate of Her worshippers and still as simple as a child's wish.

Defining the Goddess

But how do we examine a concept like the Goddess? Her essence is many-splendored and many-layered. It's complex and simple, abstract and concrete, spiritual and earthy, superhuman and human—all at the same time. When we consider the Goddess, therefore, it's like trying to get a soap bubble under a microscope. When we try to describe Her many-layered essence, it's back to paradox and extravagant language. We're trying to explain the inexplicable, and words get us only halfway there.

The mystics of the standard-brand religions go as far as they can with their pious words and esoteric diagrams, and they end up saying their god is Nothing: No Thing. That's because they don't want an earthly god. They want a god who is Pure Spirit and White Light, who is invisible and contains all things in no thing. (How? Have you ever tried to use an invisible bucket?) Omnipresent and omniscient, this god is also invariably male.[14] Many of us who worship the Goddess counter such traditional teachings by asserting that we live on a material planet, that our Goddess is *all* things, that She is pure matter.

But abstruse discussion of abstract matters gets us nowhere. I find that it's figurative language that most successfully describes the holistic concept we call "Goddess." When we talk about the Goddess, therefore, we may say she is *like* our physical mother or *like* falling rain returning to the ocean (similes), She is *the feminine principle* (metonymy, in which a part stands for the whole), She *is* the earth (both personification and metaphor). Some people say She is literally the earth; as Gaia, She embodies the planet. There are numerous metaphors: She also *is* the sun (as Amaterasu), She also *is* the moon (as Levanah), She also *is* love (as Freya), She also *is* creation (as Corn Woman). She *is* whatever we say She is, but what do we mean when we speak in figurative language? What are we really saying? As well as we can, in our halting, stumbling way, we're stating our belief in an immanent, transcendant, omnipresent Goddess.

The Goddess of the Spheres (A Metaphor)

To clarify my ideas about the Goddess, I turn to the most successful metaphor I can get my hands on, which is a set of wooden spheres. You've seen them in gift shops and catalogs: three, four, or five painted spheres, all nested one inside another. I have three or four sets of spheres, one of which is actually egg-shaped, plus a couple of orphan spheres.

The outermost sphere is generally painted midnight blue and "is" (represents) the universe. On one of my sets, the heavenly constellations are painted in gold and the astrological sun sign symbols are painted in red around the equator. The universe is the biggest, most abstract thing we think we can know; it's the "big picture." And here we are, holding it in the palm of one hand.

Split the painted universe along its equator, open it up, and discover its contents. The solar system lies nested tidily inside. In one of my sets, the solar system is deep blue-green, and the planets are circular splotches of color.

Open the solar system and the sun emerges, mirror halves with two painted faces and matching sets of golden rays. In another set the third sphere is not the sun but a two-inch earth, its oceans and continents apparently taken from renaissance maps, with Latin names and vast empty space to designate territories unexplored by Europeans: "Here be Monsters."

The innermost sphere is usually the moon, with two grace-ful painted faces and silver rays. In my egg-shaped set of five spheres (the insides of which are painted dark blue with gold stars), however, the innermost sphere is a red and gold fiery egg, complete with a tiny phoenix rising from the painted flames. In any set, the smallest sphere is the only one that's solid, the only one that doesn't contain and conceal yet another visible level of the cosmos. (Unless, of course, we include the atomic and subatomic levels of reality, in which case we can start all over again.)

If, as many of us believe or intuitively know, the Goddess "is" the cosmos, let's use our little set of painted spheres to dis-cover Her layers.

The First Sphere

As the outermost sphere represents the Goddess, then, it re-veals Her universality. It shows how She is the cosmos itself, the wholeness of creation. In the archaic creation myths, is it not the Goddess who gives birth to the stars, the suns, the moons, the planets and everything living on them? She forms everything out of clay or out of Her own body. She dances or sings or spins or weaves or shapes all things into being. In Her image are we made of clay, star stuff, or pure energy. The God-dess is the Cosmic Mother; She's the mother of the cosmos.

We can accept this as literal truth or we can understand it as figurative language; to those with faith, it makes no differ-ence. Like the myths presented in the first and second chapters of Genesis, any creation story is a testament of faith because no reporter was there to report it. The main differences between the creation myths of the standard-brand religions and the Goddess religions, of course, are the emphasis on spiritual cre-ation and the illusory nature of matter in the former and the re-ality of matter and mud in the latter, as well as the male god "giving birth" and the female goddess doing what comes naturally.

If there's a human culture in which the grandmother goddesses aren't ages older than the upstart warrior gods, it hasn't been unearthed yet. Goddesses were worshipped in Canaan long before the Hebrew tribes walked in, the sister-wives of the Hebrew Patriarchs were probably Matriarchs of the indigenous Goddess religions, and goddesses were worshipped in Jerusalem from before the time of Solomon all the way up to the Babylonian Captivity. Before there was Allah, there was Al-Lat, one of a trinity of desert goddesses; the All-Powerful One, She was worshipped as a giant granite rock.

The ancient goddesses were cosmic grandmothers, and since we have names and artifacts of goddesses from all the lands of earth, we can say that, at least in this terrestrial sense, She is universal. (Would it be straining the metaphor to call Her Madame Universe?)

Her universality has led to diversification. That is, if there's a human activity, there's a goddess to sponsor, oversee, and protect it, from birth to death, before and beyond. There are goddesses of healing, wealth, scholarship, arts and crafts, manufacture, law and justice, history and poetry, domesticity, and war.

There are goddesses of the sun, moon, sky and stars, of weather, of night and day, of the four directions, of the four elements and the seasons and time itself. There are goddesses of plantlife in general and plants in particular, likewise of the animal world and terrestrial features like mountains and springs.

There are creator goddesses, magical goddesses and shapeshifters, goddesses of all the aspects of love, ancestor goddesses and wise women, even a couple of toilet goddesses.

This is an idea we'll return to later—the diversity of the cosmic Goddess of 10,000 Names.

The Goddess of the Cosmos

Take some time now to celebrate the cosmic Goddess. You'll need something that represents the cosmos to you: your own set of nested spheres, a tektite or meteorite, an egg or a seed, a star globe or a telescope. Think big (really big) and do this ritual outdoors if you can, in the quietest place you can find. Hold your symbol of the cosmos in both hands at your navel.

Read the following words or tape them beforehand and listen to them or use them as a model to write your own words.

> She is the cosmos itself, the womb of starry seas,
> She contains all things, She bears all things.
> Inspiring and expiring, She breathes,
>> dancing on the golden solar wind,
>> broadcasting her star stuff—
>
> She is the black hole and the kitchen pantry
> She is the heartbeat of labor and love
> She is the space between the stars and atoms.
>
> She is
> She simply is
> She is whatever is
> She is What She Is
> She Is.
>
> And I am part of Her
> I Am.

Close your eyes, take several deep, easy breaths, and imagine your cosmic symbol expanding. See and feel it grow so big that it holds you in its hands at its navel. See and feel it grow so immeasurably big that you are a speck floating inside it. Now look back at your own body and see it begin to whirl and twirl, to shine and sparkle. Watch your shining, swirling self grow and grow and grow. Inhale the scent of sweet, clean solar wind, hear the sounds of thunder and the hatching of an egg, listen to the beat of a baby's rattle and the roar of the tides. See yourself grow and glow until you fill the darkness of the cosmos, until you envelop and become its emptiness, its vastness, its darkness and its light. Dark and light are in balance now, you and the cosmos are in balance, and now the balance explodes into a fountain of rainbow fireworks, a waterfall of words and sounds, a volcanic dance of living ... and then, here you are again, plain old ordinary regular you, the best beloved child of the cosmos.

When you're ready, open your eyes and spend as much time as you want examining your cosmic symbol, the earth beneath you, the sky above you.

The Goddess is, at the same time, both the cosmic creator and the created cosmos. She brings all things, visible and invisible, into existence, perhaps at the famous Big Bang or, more likely, in every instant of every day of every eon. She destroys and recycles all that She creates, including Herself. We are part of Her cosmic, universal body, we are Her thoughts made flesh, we are Her songs, Her artwork, Her psychological projection. We are Her babies.

The Second Sphere

The second sphere of our little painted set represents the solar system. It's our own neighborhood, our home, and if the solar system is home, then the heart of a home is the mother. Let's use the second layer of our metaphor, therefore, to consider the Mother Goddess and Her two other aspects, the Maiden and the Crone. Together, Maiden, Mother, and Crone are the ancient Triple Goddess, which is the oldest trinity. This is the trinity that represents the major stages of life itself as well as the stages of a woman's life.

Ever since the Greek dramatist Aeschylus made Athena say that a mother is just a sort of holding tank and hatchery for a man's sperm, making the father the real and only parent,[15] mothers have been getting a bad rap. No matter what her failings, however, our mother is our door into this world. It was through her body that we came back to earth for another opportunity to work and play. That is surely worth honor and celebration. Consider again the words you said when you did the Blessing For Our Foremothers at the beginning of this book.

To a baby, her mother (or grandmother, aunt, nurse, daycare teacher or aide, elementary school teacher, Brownie or Campfire leader) is her first goddess. To an infant, the woman who feeds and changes her, who keeps her warm and comfortable is, in fact, the whole world. To bigger, more independent kids, Mommy is still the main source of comfort and nourishment. Of course, today we also see babies without mothers, and it troubles me, a mother myself, to think about crack babies and AIDS babies, to read about babies whose mothers are still children themselves—where is the Goddess for these babies and their mothers? I wish I knew.

Nevertheless, as our mother is in some way our own original goddess, so were humankind's original goddesses their mothers and grandmothers. Perhaps they were the literal mothers and grandmothers of the clans and tribes; perhaps they were the tough old women who did the healing, counseling, and judging — the wise ones who knew where to find food, how to build shelters, how to make useful things. Their power grew with the stories told about them until they took on superhuman dimensions and people eventually began to address prayers and petitions to them.

The oldest human figures so far unearthed in Paleolithic

sites around the world are mothers—fat, fecund females like the so-called "Venuses" of Willendorf or Laussel. They're really earth mamas, 30,000 years old, and they represent the female principle of creating, procreating, mothering, nourishing, comforting, bringing rain, making the animals plentiful, both shining down and pushing up to make the crops grow. Although the people who carved and molded these figures of women with wide hips, generous stomachs, and pendulous breasts are officially termed "prehistoric" and "primitive," they were in fact highly civilized and had long oral and artistic traditions and a symbolic "language of the Goddess." If you read Marija Gimbutas's *The Civilization of the Goddess* (or even just look at the pictures), you'll see figures that will hurl you into a breathless state of respect for the minds and spirits of their creators.

Reproductions of the fat, pregnant Willendorf Mother and other Ur-Mothers are available from many sources, and I think it's helpful for us modern people to own at least one. You'll also learn something if you make your own earth mamas from clay, acrylic modeling compound, or mud.

Broadly speaking, there seem to be at least three kinds of mother goddesses:

- The queen mother, like Hera and Inanna, who may or may not actually bear children but who is sexual and fertile
- The good mother, like Demeter, Isis, and Mary, who is nearly always associated in myth or art with her daughter or son
- The terrible mother, like Kali and the grim, wicked stepmothers of all the fairy tales.

We need to be careful, however, not to let our thinking get trapped in separation and classification. If we divide and subdivide and pigeonhole the mother goddesses, we end up with a multitude of cute little figures, trivialized mommies that pack none of the old power. We've been divided and conquered, and that's one reason I think we need to look at and hold a Willendorf Mother. We need to find the old power again.

So even if what you have in your home is a specific mother goddess—a Kuan Yin or a Virgin Mary or a Crow Mother—give some thought to the holistic essence of what a mother goddess is: She is fertile. She bears children and raises them, giving rewards and punishments as deserved. And she may not have physical offspring; she can be a "mother of invention": a mother of art, music, literature, technology, discovery, industry, culture, charity, business, and anything else we can think of.

The youthful aspect of the Triple Goddess is the Mother's Daughter. Also called the Maiden or the Virgin, she is often portrayed as a little girl. She is pre-fertile, but she's fertile in her own way—as potentiality. The Maiden is (to insert a metaphor into a metaphor) the seed to her Mother's flower and her grandmother Crone's fruit.

The Maiden can represent the time of our life before we assume our adult responsibilities. She is beginnings, wildness, the wilderness. She is untouched. She is the young girl before menarche, as the Mother menstruates every month, and the post-menopausal Crone retains her "wise blood" to bear not children but power.

Like the Goddess Herself, this aspect can be hard to pin down. Sometimes she's the little girl (Kore), a virgin in the physical sense. The word "virgin" refers to more than sexual chastity and the intactness of the hymen, however; it means independence, self-determination, freedom from external ownership and control. In this sense, it's possible for a Crone to be a Virgin, and, indeed, as the wheel of existence turns and life recycles, the Crone is reborn every spring as the Virgin. Athena and Artemis are both portrayed as grownup women, but they're both virginal.

Some Virgins are sexually active. Aphrodite (also a major creation goddess) was married and the mother of several children, but she was certainly under no man's control. Perhaps she's a genuine Virgin Mother.

That's the problem with the Maiden. She's elusive. Persephone is the little daughter of Demeter, kidnapped by her uncle while she was frolicking in the meadow. Do we also remember, however, that Persephone is the awesome, dreadful Queen of the Underworld? Artemis (Diana) is the huntress, untouched by human (at least male) hands. She's also the patron of childbirth (a maternal duty) and the Queen of Heaven and Witches, and her many-breasted statue in Ephesus was one of the Wonders of the Ancient World. Are these all the same Artemis? Yes, they are; they show the all-encompassing power of the oldest goddess.

Persephone and Artemis are examples not only of the diversity of the Goddess but also of the need to keep a holistic picture in mind when we talk about the Goddess. We can focus on specific aspects for specific rituals, but realism (whatever that is) demands that we remember that She is not to be fragmented or made frivolous.

The Crone is the scariest aspect of the Triple Goddess, at least to men and in modern times when all women are desired to be forever age 19, size 2. If the Maiden is the daughter, the Crone is the grandmother, and occasionally the chaperone and babysitter. She's the old woman, and she's usually a widow, so she's the Virgin all over again. She's sometimes the Terrible Mother because she destroys life so it can be recycled. She is the Dark Mother and She is Grandmother Death, and one of her names is Hel. She's all the ugly old ones that bring justice and doom. She's the Halloween witch. She's the Grandmother of God.

The word "crone" entered the English language in 1552

and has an informative etymology: older words (in several languages) are all related to death. The Latin stem is *caro*, "flesh," and related words include "carrion," "carnage," "charnel," "carnivorous," and "excoriate," all of which give you the general idea of what a crone really is: the death goddess. It's also tempting to relate the word to Chronos and to "chronology," or time, as Mary Daly does in her *Wickedary*, where she calls the crone the "Great Hag of History" and the "long-lasting one ... who has Survived early stages of the Otherworld Journey and who has therefore discovered depths of Courage, Strength, and Wisdom in her Self."

It's popular today to hold croning ceremonies to honor older women, but it also happens that some younger women covet cronehood and insist that "it's only a state of mind." I disagree. I prefer to reserve the privilege of age and agree with other authors that a crone is a woman who has passed both the age of natural menopause and her second Saturn return (which occurs around age 56).

We're all going to grow old. Sooner or later, we'll all be Crones. We need, therefore, to consider the powers we can regain and use. We can have the wisdom based on the learning and experience of a long life; we can always learn a little more. We can find new ways to solve "mankind's" problems. The Crone may be our only hope.

The Triple Goddess is the pole star of our neighborhood. She's the little girl, a tomboy on her bike or up in a tree, a child-mother taking over the care of her siblings, a teenager in school or at the mall or out on the streets. She's the grown woman, working hard at home or in an office or plant, most likely doing two or more jobs and trying to raise her kids right and contribute something to the world in her spare time. She's the old woman, a widow in a retirement home or the neighborhood busybody keeping an eye on everything and expressing her opinions on it all. The Triple Goddess has charge of our everyday lives.

The Third Sphere

The third sphere in our little nested set is the sun. In our metaphor, this little painted sun can speak to us of warmth, nourishment, heat, and growth. It can remind us that the sun (and what it stands for: positive, projective energy, intellect, light) is not inevitably masculine; that women are smart and powerful and hot. It can also remind us that we know four dozen goddesses of the sun, from the Japanese Amaterasu to the Baltic Saule, from the ancient Arabic Shapash and the Egyptian Bast to the Cherokee Unelanúhi and Rome's Juno Lucina. Most of the sun goddesses are older than Apollo, and far less forbidding.

In other sets of spheres, the third sphere is the planet earth, and here is the emphasis I want: the earthiness of the Goddess. A few earth scientists[16] and all the earth-based religions that I know of tell us that the earth is really a living organism. Her name is Gaia, which is a variant of the old Greek name for earth, *Ge*, from which we also get "geography," "geology," and the other earthwords. Gaia, the planet, is a sentient being. The rocks and mountains are her skeleton (although some mountains, like the Paps of Anu in Ireland, are her breasts), the oceans and rivers are her blood, green plants and trees and the atmosphere are her respiratory system, either people or whales and dolphins are her brain and nervous system, and caves are her vagina and womb. We have evidence of the womblike nature of sacred caves all over the world; the cave paintings in Europe and the underground temples on the island of Malta are only two examples.

Gaia used to be able to take care of herself, adjusting her respiratory rate and temperature, for example, to bring herself back into balance in spite of her children's activities. She kept herself clean. With the indignities and overwhelming greed of the Industrial Revolution and the men who made it, however, she's been under constant attack. She's been suffering from being paved over, deep-mined and strip-mined, having bombs exploded inside her body, having her forests burned and clearcut, and from every kind of pollution people can create. Do droughts and poisoned oceans show us that she's getting weaker? Do earthquakes, volcanic eruptions, and famine indicate that she's fighting back? Many people think natural catastrophes are her way of getting our attention: *Yo! Wake up!*

Whether we take it literally or consider it to be a beautiful metaphor, the Gaia Thesis leads to ecofeminism, a basic premise of which is the connection between women and nature and the cruel abuse of both by men, especially macho men in business suits and other uniforms.

Ecofeminist theory says that as the planet is sacred *per se*, so are all things living in and on it, from mud to mountain peaks and from moose to mosquitoes. In practice, this means honoring so-called "primitive" and foreign people and not developing (and destroying) their homelands. It means working actively to make sure everyone has a place to live and enough to eat every day. It means living a kinder life, shopping cautiously, not wasting resources and energy, and recycling, repairing, and reusing. Ecofeminism can lead to changes in life on earth, a change from the usual emphasis on having power over other people and animals and plants and the ground to sharing power with them, moving from dominion over the earth to partnership with it. It can mean thinking and living not in hierarchies but in circles. It can mean leaving domination and moving into partnership.

Who is likely to initiate and work hardest to carry through such a revolution? You can bet it's not the haves and the wannabes. The revolutionaries are the intelligent women and men who bring the Goddess down from being an abstract concept into real, live action. That's *us.*

The third sphere, our little painted earth, also represents the diversity and pluralism of our goddesses. The standard-brand religions are all ferociously monotheistic: Thou shalt have no other gods—and especially no goddesses—except Me.

Goddess worshippers, on the other hand, are kind of like the old joke about Unitarians: we celebrate everyone's holidays. Deities or holidays, they're all valuable (and probably fun, too).

Some Goddess worshippers are monotheistic. There's one titanic Goddess who has a thousand names. Some of us are pantheistic. The Goddess or goddesses or both manifest everywhere and in everything, which makes everywhere and everything holy, individually and collectively. Some of us are polytheistic. There really are all those thousands of goddesses, and they're important not only to the cultures that named them but to us as well. Yes, their aspects and duties overlap, so we know 40 or 50 moon goddesses, three dozen goddesses of beauty, and great goddesses from A to Z. Not only that—we have a multitude of gods, too, all with their own names, attributes and associations, duties, and characters.

No matter what kind of ritual or spell we want to do, no matter what kind of energy we want to embody or stir into action, there's an appropriate god or goddess to invoke. Like the words in the thesaurus, however, the multitudinous gods and goddesses may be similar but none is precisely synonymous with any other. That's part of the joy of a way of life that includes the Goddess or goddesses—we have so much to play with, so many energies to work with, so much to explore.

The Innermost Sphere

The innermost sphere of our nested set is sometimes the moon, sometimes the center of the earth. I see this center as both the fire at the center of our planet and as the darkness under the ground. It's a dark fire. It's the warm darkness inside a seed or an egg, where something is germinating, waiting to be born. It's also the darkness of a warm bed where we get a good night's sleep and the grave where we dissolve into an elemental presence and wait for rebirth. Many of the ancient burial sites, in fact, reveal people curled up in fetal positions and painted with red ochre, which symbolizes menstrual blood.

At Her most basic, most elemental level, the Goddess is black fire. She is a strong dark presence, a Black Virgin Mother Crone, a black Is-ness. She's a concrete abstraction, the bright light of the dark moon. We need to reconsider the darkness, the old dark ones, the old dark ways. Our society fears and is prejudiced against this darkness. We need to balance light and dark, spirit and earth, male and female. We need to remember the forgotten old ones, the forgotten histories.[17]

It is the result of 5,000 or more years of persistent racism and sexism, and especially 300 years of determined scholarly racism that makes us believe that white is right. As far as we know, people first rose in Africa (long called the "Dark Continent") to walk on two feet, and create civilization. All the earliest peoples were small and dark. It is racism that makes us think that the tall blond people are the founders of society because they wiped out the people who had lived in the lands they now occupy. It is racism, it's hierarchical thinking, it's the focusing and overreliance on "pure" mind and the ignoring and ignorance of the "corrupt" body — it's all these that lead to the ages-old dichotomies that seem to rule our world. Over and over, we hear that:

white = good / black = bad
white male = good / black anyone = bad
male = good / female = bad

mind = male = good / body = female = bad
white light = God = good / darkness = the Devil = evil
spirit = light = God = good / earth = darkness = the Devil = bad

Even a scientist, Linda Jean Shepherd, compares diversity of thought to "the many-colored veil" of Isis. When we're forced to choose only this one or that one, to rank this one above that one, the many-colored veil, she says, is reduced to black and white. In society, in science, in the arts, in schools and corporations, even in the New Thought, we're led to think that the world is a true/false test, whereas reality is truly multiple-choice play.

It's this binary kind of thinking that created empires in "uncivilized" lands where people had been living and thriving for thousands of years. It's this kind of thinking that encourages genocide and enslaves people. Wrapping things or people in Pure White Light to "purify" them can be racist, sexist, and imperialist.

My goddess is the cosmic mother who enfolds the universe, the ordinary woman, and the quiet dark fire at the center of the holy planet we live on—all at the same time.

Let me say it another way. Here's an excerpt from one of my forthcoming novels. This scene takes place in the house of a Neolithic shaman who lives in Old Europe:

Another figure now began to take shape, forming from dust motes and ashes and the darkness beneath the red of the fire.

She stood before them, as tall and deep and black as boundless space, as calm and wise and dark as the fertile earth. Her skin shone with purple and green and gold lights and She wore a crescent moon upon Her forehead, or perhaps it was two horns around which Her hair seemed to writhe. Around Her broad, muscular body lay the double helix of two vast serpents, their heads resting just above Her full breasts. The full moon shone in Her hair, and they saw the stars in Her skin.

She held both hands out toward her children.

I have actually seen this goddess. When I suffered a severe asthma attack in June 1992, and was rushed by two of my circle sisters to the emergency room, I lost consciousness at the door and was "gone" for twenty minutes. She was with me then. Although I later created a collage in which I tried to show Her, it hardly comes close, and I also lack the words to adequately describe Her.

And, finally, there's one last layer of the Goddess, one that slips through all the metaphors. Sometimes she's named Eris, who is the "patron saint" of chaos theory. She's also the one who manifests as all the found goddesses, like Asphalta (for parking spaces), Chocolata and Vibrata (two goddesses of ecstasy), and the domestic goddesses: Roseanne the Terrible, Refrigerata the Preserver, and the tiny but powerful Micro-Waveleh. Her kid brother is Coyote the Trickster.

You get the idea.

I call her the Goddess Gotcha. Gotcha has the strong sense of humor we all need to survive in this ridiculous civilization, and she has scant patience with pomposity and pride. Gotcha is the one who sends the cats in with their jingle toys when you're doing a high, holy ritual and everyone's taking themselves entirely too seriously. Gotcha makes you tongue-tangled when your invocation goes on too long, and she plants puns and double-entendres in your reading and typos in your writing. The only thing to do when she appears is to greet her: Hail, Gotcha, Fulla Fun and Outta Sight.

She may be the most potent goddess of them all, and you'll find a ritual to honor her following Chapter 7. First, let's do a ritual to honor the fullness of the Goddess in all women.

A Ritual to Celebrate the Goddess in Women

For this ritual, you need your usual private space and something to make noise with—a doumbek or frame drum, a rattle,
two sticks you can beat together, or your own hands to clap.[18]
Beat or clap as long as you want to whenever you come to the
cue [Sound].

Before you begin the chant, imagine a bright, pulsing
stream of spring green light moving in a clockwise direction
around your body. See and feel it start in the area of your heart
and just let it go round and round for a few minutes. Don't
force the light, and don't hurry this part of the ritual.

After a few minutes, let the light become strong enough to
make you sway in tiny circles with it. When this circling is well
established, turn the light into a green helix that spirals around
your whole body, round and round from the top of your head to
the base of your spine (if you're sitting) or your heels (if you're
standing). Really feel this energy, feel its warmth and strength,
let your body sway in its wind. Take as long as necessary to get
the helix established so it can run on automatic while you do
the chant. (If you're new at this, yes, it *is* real energy and, yes, it
will keep going while you concentrate on the words.)

Read the following words or record them beforehand and
listen to them or use them as a pattern to make up your own
words. Women should say "I am" and men should say "She is"
(or whatever the appropriate verb is) throughout this chant.

> I am/She is the powerful one. [Sound]
> I can do whatever must be done. [Sound]
>
> I can create new life. [Sound]
> Through my body, under my heart
>   children come to earth, people come to life. [Sound]
> Through my mind, because of my will

ideas come to life, material takes new form. [Sound]
I can do whatever must be done. [Sound]

I can build and I can tame
I can plant and I can tend. [Sound]
I am powerful
I can do whatever must be done. [Sound]
I can go forward and I can resist
I can caress and I can be angry. [Sound]
I am powerful
I can do whatever must be done. [Sound]

I can nourish and I can punish
I can preserve and I can celebrate. [Sound]
I am powerful
I can do whatever must be done. [Sound]

I am the darkness and the light
I am the word and the dance
I am the growth and the harvest. [Sound]
I am power
I will do whatever must be done. [Sound]

At the end of the chant, make as much sound as you can. You can also repeat lines of the chant that you want to hear coming from your mouth again.

When the energy gets as strong as you want it to be, direct the sounds into the spiraling green light, and then direct the light into your spine. Let it move up and down your spine for about one minute, then take several deep breaths and lie down, put the palms of your hands flat on the ground or floor, and allow all this energy to drain into the earth. If you feel light-headed, lie still a while longer, and when you get up, eat something made of grain (crackers, tortillas, pretzels, popcorn, bread, etc.) and drink some water.

This ritual is wonderful when it is done by a group of women (only) on the night of the full moon. You'll *know* you embody the Goddess!

PART TWO

UNENCUMBERED RITUAL

UNENCUMBERED
RITUAL

You can make it a really big deal. You can do research in a dozen authoritative books. Build a 12-foot-tall Goddess. Set up and decorate your altar with pomp and ceremony, using the prescribed symbols for the four directions and properly sanctified altar implements. Light beeswax candles in the proper colors and anointed with the proper sacred oils. Burn specially prepared incense. Plan, write, and rehearse the scripted invocations, chants, and music. Hire a dozen drummers and flutists. Choreograph all movement. Coordinate your ritual with the phase of the moon, the movements of the planets, the time of day, the day of the week, and the season of the year. Create spectacular robes and costumes, masks and jewelry for all participants. Find a mind-blowing location with privacy, a spectacular view, growing trees, blooming flowers, and perhaps a mountain in the background. Invite 30 or 40 of your closest friends.

It takes a lot of work to pull off a really great ritual that pulls in genuine power, and it's truly worth every bit of work you do. It can change your life.

Most of us are solitaries, however; we worship alone most of the time and just don't have the time, energy, financial means, and other resources to enact a really big ritual very often. Our rituals are more likely to be little private ones that we create on the spot to celebrate a private achievement or to ask for help. We light a candle, talk to the appropriate goddess, and maybe do a brief meditation or just sit quietly and at peace for a few minutes.

This is what I call *unencumbered ritual.* It's not fancy. It doesn't follow the official rules and take a lot of stuff. It may not even look like a real ritual. But it works. It's repeatable and it alters your consciousness. It's very personal, and the emotional content is fully satisfying. The rituals we've already done in this book were unencumbered rituals.

Magic

Elaborate or unencumbered, ritual gives us another M-word to consider: when we do a ritual, we're making magic.

Let's get clear about one point right away. Magic is not black or white or even gray. The racist, sexist society we've been living in for at least a millenium has determined that white = good and black = bad. Black magic is bad, white magic is good, and gray magic is a cop-out. Actually, magic comes in all the colors of the rainbow, and can perhaps best be categorized by the colors associated with the chakras.[19] As I see them, the rituals in this book are many-colored.

Possibly the most famous definition of magic is Dion Fortune's: it's the art of changing consciousness at will. Starhawk adds that it's "the art of evoking power-from-within ... the act that releases the mysteries" of the living universe. Magic, which is mysterious in both senses of that word, is what helps us change our world.

Magic is education. It's like going to school, where we drill in the multiplication tables, learn vocabulary and grammar, write essays and term papers, train our muscles and learn teamwork, and perform scientific experiments. When we study magic and begin to do rituals, we have to drill in elemental correspondences, learn the vocabulary and grammar of magic, recreate or invent Goddess stories, exercise our intellectual and emotional muscles, work with other powers or people, and perform scientific experiments (called "spells"). School is supposed to prepare us to live better in the objective, everyday world; magic not only prepares us to live better in this world, but it also gives us access to the world where things happen before they manifest here. It's art and science combined to strengthen our intellectual and emotional powers and our will for the performance of specific tasks. The work and its results sometimes appear to be supernatural.

But you won't learn to do any knock-'em-dead tricks by reading this book, nor will you get a course of instruction in "miracles" or in developing your will so you can make people obey you. My primary goals are worship and celebration; the magic and the power come along with the changes in your consciousness. People probably won't even notice how powerful you're becoming, and you won't care because you're doing this for yourself and to help heal the consciousness of the planet.

It disturbs me to hear words like "power" and "will" used carelessly. They're words that stand for major issues in our world, and people throw them around without definition. As I use "power," it's nearly synonymous with "energy." Energy is unfocused potential, and power is energy put to work. It's directed by my will, which is my goal or purpose, my *magical intention*.

Power and will can be "positive" or "negative," "helpful" or "unhelpful," "good" or "bad," "valid" or "invalid." These eight words are in quotation marks because they're so slippery. They lie along a continuum and slide back and forth all over it, depending on who's using them, and why. The underlying issues are "power over" other people or "power with" people, plus *whose* will.[20] Many people say "God's will" when they mean "my will," for example, and others try to overpower any group they work with.

To make it more slippery, we can put the two words together: "will power." I studied for a year or so with a "spiritual therapeutic" school (founded by a European psychiatrist) that teaches that only God above can have will and power, or will power; that people shouldn't even say "I want," because everything on earth is illusory: the only reality is God's will and power, so there's nothing real here that we can want.

Huh??

I find this kind of teaching extremely poisonous, especially to women and people of color. We haven't been permitted to have wills of our own for several thousand years. A willful girl, for example, is a naughty girl; she'll never catch a husband. A willful (fill in our own ethnic epithet) is uppity and needs to be taught a lesson.

We need to regain and express our wills. We must regain and express our feminine and cultural powers. It's OK to say, "My will be done" and know that we mean it and that other people understand what we're saying.

As always, of course, there are limits: "My will be done" should not cross the line into power over. When that happens, we assume the characteristics of the people who have been our abusers.

An overreaching "my will be done" can also lead to arrogance and guruism. I once met a woman who led rituals and who told me that a little after 5 P.M. on October 17, 1989, she was doing magic with a diamond ring that had been in her Bay Area family for several generations. She's bitter about how her family has treated her, diamonds are known to store and magnify great amounts of power, and so—voila! She caused the San Francisco earthquake! I prefer to believe that she was merely trying to impress me and that she doesn't really take responsibility for a major earthquake just because she's mad at her parents and knows something about magic.

As I see it, then, developing our magical will and using magical power help us better understand ourselves and the universe and lead us back to worship of the Goddess in Her many layers. If we lack will and power, we'll never get anywhere because we lack purpose and energy. If we lack willpower, we don't know where we're going, and someone else is probably in charge of our lives anyway. Whether we study multiplication or magic, therefore, we should learn to express and assert ourselves, but without running over other people.

And it's not helpful to do a ritual and then sit around waiting for the miracles to rain down upon us. As a friend once said while we were doing a ritual together, "Trust the Goddess and do your own homework." All the ritual books say the same thing. If we want more money, for example, we should do money rituals and burn green candles to focus our will and stir up a little personal power (self-esteem). Then we need to get out and see what we can do to earn that money. The Goddess will meet us halfway: a client or a job will "just happen" to be where we can find it.

A Ritual of Personal Power

These words, which came to me at four o'clock one morning, reveal the context of our personal power: the elements of the universe, the light and the dark, the Goddess herself. That is to say, the universe is a hologram and we're part of it, and the power any of us has is part of that holographic power.

To find out for yourself, and to bring something into your

life as well, do this ritual any time. Use four candles in colors you like or feel to be powerful. State your intention where indicated. This intention can be fairly specific ("Bring XX into my life" or "Help me understand this situation") or general ("I want to feel better today").

By the powers of the cleansing fires,
By the powers of the springing tides,
By the powers of the soaring winds,
By the powers of the growing earth,
[State your intention or affirmation]
    Let my will be done. [Light first candle]

By the powers of the rising sun,
By the powers of the changing moon,
By the powers of the dancing planets,
[Repeat your intention or affirmation]
    Let my will be done. [Light second candle]

By the powers of the shining light,
By the powers of the sheltering dark,
[Repeat your intention or affirmation]
    Let my will be done. [Light third candle]

By the powers of the living Goddess,
[Repeat your intention or affirmation]
    Let my will be done. [Light fourth candle]

Sit quietly in the glow of the candlelight and consider what you and the universe can do when you work together on some goal.

4

LOOKING AT
THE TRADITIONS

Ten or twenty years ago, when this new/old religion we're creating was still half fantasy, we used to hear a lot about "traditions," many of which claimed roots either directly divine or passed down from Ancient Masters in Atlantis or Shamballah or wherever, roots that were at the very least medieval. It seems to me that once upon a time we needed such claims. Being able to say that we, too, had roots gave us increased respectability among the other neopagans.

I look at words with skeptical, pedantic eyes, however. Like you, I've learned that you can't always believe what people proclaim, no matter how earnest they are. And when we do a bit of serious research, we learn that most (but not all) of these "traditions" are younger than I am. (I was born in July of 1941.) You can, for example, read about the creation of the Gardnerian "tradition" in 1939 in Doreen Valiente's *Witchcraft for Tomorrow*, and other books reveal that Gardner and his associates spent much of the 1940s and 1950s rewriting their Book of Shadows to make it *sound medieval*, turning modern English into something old-Englishy. I know people who are still creating traditions today. Nearly every day, in fact. Now I am *not* putting any person or tradition down. I think it's a good idea to create new traditions. Multiplicity is terrific.

As I see it, the multitudinous neopagan traditions are comparable to the multitude of Protestant denominations. Pagan or Christian, they all share a few common overarching beliefs, but each one believes and worships in its idiosyncratic ways. It seems to me that Gardnerian Wicca, with its roots in ceremonial magic and British Rosicrucianism, is analogous to High Church Anglican Catholicism: it's the most orthodox of our "traditions." Other traditions are analogous to other denominations, and each one believes that its way is The Right Way To Do It.[21] And even though the various believers tolerate other ways, I bet they're all secretly hoping for conversions.

In the various Witchy, Wiccan, Crafty, and Neo-Pagan "traditions," therefore, rituals can be pretty strictly organized. Each tradition, coven, circle, or school has its own structure, although minor variations are sometimes admitted. Many groups rely on a Book of Shadows, which contains the outlines and scripts for the major sabbats (the eight festivals of the year), new and full moon rituals, and special rituals like initiation and handfasting (marriage). A Book of Shadows also records other wisdom, like spells (with expected results), recipes for incenses and oils, diagrams for arranging the altar for each ritual, and pertinent information on the use of the tools: salt, water, pentacle, sword or knife, wand, chalice, candles, incense, etc.

It's virtually impossible to do a comprehensive survey of ritual practice, however, because some groups are closed and keep all their rituals private and highly secret. Some groups hold occasional open rituals (open to especially invited guests or to the general public, depending on the occasion) but they keep the important rituals secret. And some groups hardly ever do the same thing twice. Where the ritual is held also affects its structure (you can't do a spiral dance in someone's living room), and open rituals probably differ from closed ones.

Still, based on research and conversations with people who do regular rituals, I can make a few generalizations. There are seven procedural steps that seem to be common:

1. **Purification.** Assuming that cleansing is needed, incense, saltwater, or visualization is used to purify people and tools. Sometimes the space is purified as well.

2. **Casting the circle.** The circle is cast, or closed, by calling in the powers of the four (or six or seven) directions, the four elements, the Goddess, and sometimes the God. This is sometimes done by the priestess and her assistant, sometimes by members of the group. When the circle has been cast, it usually means that no one is permitted to come in or go out, though I've been in circles where people wander back and forth at will.

3. **Stating the intention.** This is the purpose of the gathering, its will to be done. It can be a sabbat celebration, healing, working for world and personal peace, a prosperity ritual, or any other special occasion.

4. **Raising power.** The group chants, sings, or makes music by drumming and clapping, does a prescribed dance, or silently visualizes the rising power. The raised power is often referred to as a "cone of power."

5. **Trance work or visualization.** The priestess or priest leads a guided meditation that uses the power just raised for a specific purpose. Sometimes the cone of power is aimed and sent out to a specific target.

6. **Grounding the energy.** The energy must be returned to the earth.

7. **Opening the circle.** All invisible powers are thanked and sent back to where they came from and the people adjourn for refreshment and a social hour.

You're likely to find instructions on these basic steps, combined or subdivided or in a different order, in almost every book on ritual. Sometimes the people "check in" first, bringing everyone else up to date on how their lives have been going and how they're presently feeling. Checking in can include self-introductions, too, if guests are present or the group is full of irregular attendees. Sometimes the intention is stated before the circle is cast. People working in the Gardnerian traditions read the Charge of the Goddess and draw down the full moon—or at least its power—into the high priestess and thence into the circle. Not every ritual includes trance work, and many groups celebrate the sabbats by staging dramatic rituals and acting out the appropriate mythological story.

These are rituals for groups, of course, but solitaries in the traditions try to follow the same outlines, doing all the steps by themselves at their home altars. One purpose of this book is to give such people other kinds of rituals to add to their traditions.

A "Traditional" New Moon Ritual

To give us a point of comparison between "traditional" and unencumbered ritual, let's visit a new moon ritual. This is a fictitious, generic ritual group (though it is fairly typical of ritual groups) and is not intended to portray any specific people or "traditions" or give away any secrets. Notice that its members are regular people dealing with the same issues you and I deal with every day.

It's dusk, the first new moon of the early spring and just about a week before the spring equinox.

Rituals of this coven, Our Lady of the Clear Skies, are customarily done in Helen's house. Helen, who holds a B.A. in art history, works in a restaurant because she was divorced six years ago when her husband found someone younger and slimmer. Trained in a Gardnerian coven 20 years ago, she received the lowest degree of initiation but became a mainstream Protestant when she married. After her Episcopalian husband died five years ago, she returned to the Goddess religion when she "just happened" to meet an old friend in a metaphysical bookstore. She gradually drew people to her, and this coven was formed two years ago. There are six faithful attendees and another five or six who come when they don't have other commitments.

The first woman to arrive is Angela, a ferocious feminist who works as a bookkeeper in an aerospace firm. Her partner, Lynn, is at a Greenpeace demonstration tonight and they have promised to send energy to each other. Angela checks this out with Helen and they agree to ask the group about it.

Angela helps Helen set up the altar against the north wall of Helen's living room. The others come in gradually in ones and twos. One is Marie, a housewife whose husband of 23 years is in the Persian Gulf for the duration.[22] The other is Harry, who works at a computer store in one of the local malls. He tells the women how glad he is to be off tonight. Marie takes her homemade pound cake into the kitchen and Harry sits down to watch the women arrange the altar.

The next covener to arrive is Lavender, an aging California hippie with long, scarlet hair. All her life, she has been mystically attracted to nature, and she lives with 47 plants, three cats, two dogs, two parakeets, a snake, her daughter by her second husband, and her boyfriend, Marc, who is parking the car. He's attending law school and attends rituals when he's not overwhelmed with his studies.

The last to arrive tonight, just barely in time and complaining about traffic and lack of convenient parking, are Peggy, Madelyn, and Louisa. Peggy, an incest survivor, barely survives on temp work as a clerk-typist and attends five 12-step programs a week. She is a nervous woman who recently quit smoking. Madelyn is a marketing communications manager in a mid-size development company that may not survive the recession. Though no one is supposed to know it, she helps Peggy out financially from time to time. Louisa works as a computer programmer and is trying to find a job with better pay and benefits before another round of layoffs hits her company. She also creates Goddess art and sells enough to make a small profit.

Realizing that feelings are high tonight, Helen wraps a silver and green shawl around her shoulders and says, "Let's get started now." As everyone joins hands to make a semicircle facing the altar, she adds, "Why don't we all just breathe for a few minutes?" She starts a tape of ocean sounds and takes her place at the right end of the semicircle. They all close their eyes, and within two or three minutes they're breathing deeply in unison.

When she's satisfied that everyone is fully present and focused, Helen drops Harry's hand and goes to the altar. First she raises the ritual chalice, one of a set of Waterford goblets she received as a wedding present. It's half full of bottled water. She holds the chalice in both hands above her head.

"Creature of water, be thee present here. I exorcise thee and bid thee cast all impurities out of this sacred space. In the Names of Isis and Aditi—blessed be."

The circle repeats, "Blessed be."

Helen replaces the chalice on the altar and lifts a small raku bowl of coarse sea salt. "Creature of salt, bless this circle. Let only good enter herein. In the Names of Isis and Aditi—blessed be."

"Blessed be."

She drops a pinch of salt into the water and swirls it in a clockwise direction as the salt dissolves. Next she lights the two white beeswax altar candles.

Finally she picks up her athame, a black-handled knife with a four-inch blade, and nods to Marie and Angela. They step forward. Angela picks up the chalice and Marie picks up the incense, a single stick in a little wood holder. As Helen walks to the eastern boundary of the circle and raises her athame above her head, everyone faces east.

"Hail, Guardians of the Watchtowers of the East, Powers of Air. Rising sun, cleansing winds, Ninlil, Mistress of the Winds—by the air that is Her breath, be here now!"[23]

Marie raises the incense, "By the powers of fire and air, I purify the East." Angela raises the chalice. "By the powers of earth and water, I bless the East."

Everyone murmurs, "Blessed be," and the three women walk behind the coven to the south boundary of the circle, stopping behind Marc. Everyone faces south.

"Hail, Guardians of the Watchtowers of the South, Powers of Fire. Warmth of noon, cleansing flames, Pele, Mistress of Fire—by the fire that is Her spirit, be here now!"

Marie and Angela repeat their blessings, the group seals the south with a "Blessed be," and the three women walk to the western boundary of the circle, stopping behind Louisa. Everyone faces west and Helen raises her athame a third time.

"Hail, Guardians of the Watchtowers of the West, Powers of Water. Shade of twilight, cleansing tides, Yemaya, Mistress of the Seas—by the waters of Her living womb, be here now!"

Marie and Angela repeat their blessings again, the group seals the west with a "Blessed be," and the three women walk to the altar. Helen raises her athame a fourth time.

"Hail, Guardians of the Watchtowers of the North, Powers of Earth. Silence of midnight, sacred earth, Ceres, Mistress of Grain—by the earth that is Her body, be here now!"

After Marie and Angela bless the north, Helen traces a link back to the east with her athame, sealing the circle. As her assistants place their implements back on the altar and return to the semicircle, Helen closes her eyes and bows her head for a minute.

"The circle is cast, the energy is sealed, and we are once more in the place between the worlds. This is the place that is no place, where all things meet in honor and blessing, where birth and death, light and dark, joy and sorrow, and coming and going are as one." She touches the point of her athame to the painted wooden pentacle on the altar, then lays the knife on the altar. She walks back to Harry and kisses him lightly on the cheek, saying, "In perfect trust, may this kiss be passed around the cir-

cle." *Harry kisses Peggy and repeats the blessing, and Peggy turns to the next member of the coven until the blessing is passed around the circle.*

At Helen's gesture they all sit down on the floor. "We're here tonight," *she says calmly,* "to celebrate the new moon. The moon is transiting Aries tonight, which means we're entering a two-day period of self-assertion, self-expression, and busyness. This is a time to start new projects —"

"Oh, good," *Louisa interrupts.* "Maybe that means I'll get that job at WardCo!" *Everyone nods and makes encouraging sounds and Helen smiles.*

"Since there's so much going on with us and in the whole world," *she continues,* "and the new moon is the time of beginnings, I want to do a special kind of healing tonight." *They all nod.* "Not just a physical healing, though let's give Peggy more energy to keep her away from cigarettes —"

"Three days and 11 hours," *Peggy whispers.*

"Good for you!" *Harry says, and Madelyn hugs her.*

"And let's send more energy to Harry's AIDS buddy, who is in the hospital again," *Helen continues.* "Mostly, though, let's channel healing energy to Dennis to keep him safe and bring him home —" *Marie closes her eyes and touches her wedding ring.* "And let's do a healing for peace on earth."

After some heated discussion, the coven agrees that healing energy can only help the issues at hand and that they will do their part.

"Well, good," *Helen says.* "So let's try it this way. We'll raise a nice green cone of power and send it straight up, and then we can each send a ray of it wherever we want it to go. Okay? I'm sure that'll work, though I don't think I've ever heard of anyone doing it quite that way before."

There are a few smiles, and Helen reaches for her doumbek,[24] which sits next to the altar. This is a hammered copper, womb-shaped drum, and she cradles it under her left arm, resting the head on her thigh. Lavender picks up her frame drum, which is decorated with beads and feathers, and they all begin the chant. The two drums beat slowly at first, the "motherbeat," then pick up speed as the chant accelerates from single vowel sounds to Goddess names to statements of intention. Guided by Helen, who is visualizing an emerald green meteor flying around above their heads, they finally reach a climax, "Peace! Peace! Peace on earth! Peace be with us! Peace! Peace! Peace! Heal! Heal! Heal the earth!"

There is a fury of drumbeats, then sudden silence, and the coven visualizes the green cone rising into the sky above Helen's house. Rays of emerald light fly off, directed at specific targets until, in their imaginations at least, the entire sky is green and the green light blankets the planet.

"As we will it," Helen whispers, "so may it be done. Peace and healing for the earth and all peoples, now and forever. So mote it be."

"So mote it be," the coven affirms, repeating the ancient blessing that means, "Amen, so be it."

"Watch the green light moving into the Federal Building," Helen murmurs as the coven sits with their eyes closed. "Let us work in peace for peace. Watch the green light move into our own homes and give us peace and healing in whatever ways we need it. Now watch the healing green light encircle the earth and shine on the desert 8,000 miles around the planet, where Marie's husband waits. Let it touch him and all the men and women stationed there, and let it touch the hearts of all people in that part of the world, no matter what god they worship. Let it touch the forests, the sea, the stricken land, let it transform the fishing industry against which Lynn is working tonight."

Helen touches her drum again and a barely audible drumbeat fills the room, heartbeats made palpable, as each coven member visualizes the working of his or her own green cone of power. Finally, there is silence, and they can all feel their energy flowing back into the earth beneath them, grounding them and bringing them peace, too.

After several minutes, arms and legs begin to stretch, mouths yawn and eyes open, and Helen knows their work has succeeded. When she judges that everyone is ready, she lays the drum aside and stands up, adjusting her shawl, "Are we ready to open the circle?"

They all get to their feet and join hands, and Helen walks to the center. She raises her athame and faces each direction as she addresses it.

"Guardians of the Watchtowers of the North, all Powers of Earth, we do thank you for being present in our circle tonight. Return now to your realms in peace. Hail and farewell.

"Guardians of the Watchtowers of the West, all Powers of Water, we do thank you for being present in our circle tonight. Return now to your realms in peace. Hail and farewell.

"Guardians of the Watchtowers of the South, all Powers of Fire, we do thank you for being present in our circle tonight. Return now to your realms in peace. Hail and farewell.

"Guardians of the Watchtowers of the East, all Powers of Air, we do thank you for being present in our circle tonight. Return now to your realms in peace. Hail and farewell.

"Our circle is open but never broken. May the peace and love of the Goddess encircle the earth. Merry meet, merry part, and merry meet again."

The members of the group all hug each other with genuine affection, Helen and Marie bring the refreshments in from the kitchen, and they all spend another hour together, catching up on gossip, plans, and hopes.

This is not a real ritual nor are these real people. It is, however, a realistic portrayal. The coven is depicted with its various relationships, and discussion and consensus are used to solve problems.

Helen is the leader not because she's the smartest or the oldest, but because she knows the most. (She's obviously read *The Spiral Dance* and other books on ritual.) She's also training the others, and sometimes Angela or Harry or another member serves as priestess or priest and prepares and leads a ritual. That's because Helen learned an important lesson a long time ago: if you hold all the power yourself and do all the work yourself, you'll wear out and the others will become resentful. It's as true around an altar as it is around a conference table.

Before I move on to the next chapters and begin explaining how you can simplify the rituals you do alone or with a few friends, let's review the general elements of this ritual.

Purification

The first thing Helen did was to tame the tensions the people brought in with them. She asked them to breathe in unison, which has an automatic calming effect. These people have been meeting together for a few years, so it takes only a couple of silent minutes. With people who were less intimate or in a more troublesome situation, she could have begun with a brief visualization in which she guided them to see their tensions draining out through toes and fingertips into the earth. She could have used a specially mixed incense burned on self-igniting charcoal and fanned its cleansing smoke into each person's aura. Because Peggy is a new nonsmoker, however, Helen wants to keep smoke to a minimum. This is also important to remember if anyone in the group is asthmatic or otherwise sensitive to smoke. (As a chronic asthmatic myself, I always make sure I sit upwind.)

Purifying water and salt is an old practice, used by ceremonial magicians[25] and covens in the Gardnerian tradition and also adopted by some other Witches. I find it significant that it's the two feminine elements, water and earth (salt), that are used to banish intruders and purify the circle.

You can also do a purification silently and use other tools. Smudge, which is very popular these days, is a bundle of sage, cedar, and other herbs tied with string. One end of the smudge stick is lit and waved in the air; the smoke can also be fanned into each person's aura with a feather.

If you want to avoid smoke, pass a half-full chalice around

the circle, letting each person visualize his or her tribulations draining into the water. Pour the water on the ground, or at least down a drain, after the ritual. You can also stroke each person's aura downward with a feather, a flower or leafy branch, a bunch of herbs, or a cotton or silk scarf. Follow the stroking with a "blessed be" or a light kiss.

Casting the Circle

The "Guardians of the Watchtowers" are more holdovers from ceremonial magic. They're also referred to as the "Lords of the Watchtowers" and frequently visualized as mighty archangels bearing their fiery swords before them. In some traditions, the priest or priestess carries the ritual sword around the boundary of the circle to demarcate the space.

If you want a less martial effect, invoke goddesses or gods, or both, that are associated with the directions and elements. I'll discuss the directions and their elements and alternate invocations in greater detail in Chapters 5 and 6.

Instead of having one person do all of the directional invocations, you can ask a person sitting in each direction to invoke its powers. You can point to the direction with a wand, a feather, a flower or leafy branch, or your own hands. You can do it sitting down and without turning to face each direction.

As far as I've been able to learn, the phrase "Blessed be" was created by Gerald Gardner and his associates. It's not a "traditional blessing" in the sense that Witches have been saying it to each other for a thousand years. It does, however, have literary antecedents. Fantasizing about getting away from London and returning to the countryside, eighteenth-century English poets like John Dryden wrote "Beatus ille" poems; the Latin word *beatus* means "blessed" and *beatus ille means* "blessed is he." This, of course, reminds us of the Beatitudes (Matthew 5:3–11), which begin "Blessed are the poor."

Stating the Intention

Whether you're working alone or in a group, always be sure to *say out loud* why you're doing this ritual. You can't be focused if you're not clear about what you're focusing on.

Helen took advantage of the special new moon energy of beginnings to begin a healing and to state a many-branched intention. She also used the Aries transit to give it extra power. Even if, like me, you don't really speak astrologese, you can use an astrological calendar to track the celestial energies and time your own rituals to take advantage of them. Don't be a slave to astrology, however; you can do any ritual anytime. When you state your intention aloud, it lets both the universe at large and your own subconscious know what you've got in mind, whatever the prevailing energies may be.

Keeping in mind the inalterable fact that what you put out comes back at least threefold, you can create a ritual with any intention, from attracting and drawing health and love into your life to banishing those who develop open lands and hexing a rapist or other abuser of women and children. Banishing and hexing are very controversial topics; such rituals are often called "negative" and "manipulative," and some writers say you should never, ever do such things. I believe that we can do banishing and hexing (see Chapter 11), but we must do it without anger and state aloud and with absolute clarity that what we're doing is returning negative energy to the sender. We're sending back what that abuser has himself already put out. We are, in other words, acting as a mirror, reflecting garbage rays back to their originator.

Raising Power

You can use the chants given in Chapter 2. You can also make up anything else that works, including pure vowel sounds, or you can drum. Repetition and rhythm are what power the chants and alter your consciousness.

Even though you may not be able to see it, it's real energy you're working with. As they say, you can't see electricity either, or the wind, but you know they're there and use their power all the time. (Invisible power is described in Chapter 6.)

As I suggested in the ritual at the end of Chapter 3, it helps to consciously visualize the energy and get it moving into the pattern you want. Once you get it moving, it will keep going while you concentrate on other things. If you want to, you can check back in on it from time to time. You'll see—it'll still be spinning or circling.

Containing the raised and focused power is the reason that you cast the circle and don't let people break it. (Animals and small children seem to cause no interruptions in the flow of the energy, however much they may interrupt you.) It's like you're mixing batter for a cake. You've got to put the flour and the eggs and the other ingredients into a bowl, one that is big enough to contain all the energy, because if you don't, when you put the electric mixer into it, you'll have batter all over you, all over the counter and the cabinets, all over the walls and floor. You'll have a mess to clean up and no cake to eat. Your ritual energy is the batter of your cosmic cake.

Helen guided the energy with both her mind and her drum. Her mind focused and guided it, and the drum beats gave it rhythm, which set up a wave pattern. The wave pattern catches all the individual energies of the individual people and brings them into resonance, or entrainment, which magnifies the power. Listen to any chant, from "No blood for oil" to "Two, four, six, eight, who do we appreciate?" It has regular beats. People clap or stomp or wave their banners to the rhythm and pretty soon everyone's shouting in unison. It's hard, in fact, to get out once you're entrained. You become one with the group.

Think of the power of other rhythmic ways you raise energy. One of them can result in babies.

Trance Work or Visualization

No matter what you did to raise that power, the power alters your state of consciousness. Your will is focused, and extraneous things are set aside for the moment. You are truly in the place between the worlds, and this is the place where things happen before they manifest in our everyday consciousness and in our ordinary lives.

When we do trance work or visualization, we're in a hypnotic state. The naive, childlike subconscious that lives in our hearts behind our walls of sophistication and cynicism is now open for unfiltered communication. It believes what we show or tell it and works simply and powerfully (if also sometimes slowly and deviously).

Helen could have asked another member of the group to lead the visualization, and it could have taken a more concrete form. They could have visualized Concordia, the Roman goddess of peace, infusing all sources of conflict with a will for peace. The only limit to a visualization is your fearless, active imagination, and the more outrageous an image is, the more effective it is at grabbing the energy and running with it.

Grounding the Energy

It is vital to ground the energy you raise. You *must* ground it. If you don't, you'll probably be jittery for days and toss and turn all night. One good way to ground the energy that your ritual has raised is to visualize the energy draining out of your body through your hands and feet and the base of your spine, down through furniture and floors and buildings, and burrowing into the earth, where it is absorbed and recycled.

You also need to ground yourself after you leave the ritual. I often ground myself after a ritual by washing dishes or doing some other homely chore. I can do this easily because I work at home and do many of my rituals before noon to take advantage of the rising power of the sun. Scrubbing dishes or the toilet really brings one back to earth, and remember—that's how Brother Lawrence practiced the presence of his god. You don't have to wash dishes after you get home from a ritual, but you may want to read awhile before you go to bed.

Group hugs and refreshments and a social hour also help us ground energies and prepare us to go back out into a world that may not understand what we're all about.

Opening the Circle

Helen used a somewhat simplified version of opening the circle. Instead of standing in the center, she could have walked to each direction again. There are all sorts of reasons for using a simpler closing, from being a bit unsteady on your feet to having to go to the bathroom *now*. (Here's an idea for casting the circle: make it as big as your whole home so you can go to the bathroom and the kitchen without violating the boundaries.)

Please keep in mind that, unlike the medieval demonologists like Dr. Faustus and some ceremonial magicians, we haven't summoned the presence of the invisible powers so we can command them and put them to work for us. We've invited them to be present so we can all work together. (It's that issue of "power over" and "power with" again.) That means that when we open the circle, we don't banish the invisibles. We thank them for being with us for our ritual.

Always treat the invisibles with respect, whether they're your own mental and emotional powers, elemental spirits and devas, or angels and goddesses. Even if you can't see them, they're real, and you never quite know what they can do and when they might do it. You don't want to antagonize a god or a salamander (elemental fire spirit) or an archangel.

If you don't object to invisible powers hanging around with you, you can also say something like, "Go if you must or stay if you will." This gives the spirit the option. Be aware, however, that you may not be interesting enough for an invisible to hang around with for very long.

"Merry meet ..." is another "traditional" saying, both benediction and promise.

5

ALTERING
YOUR ALTAR

You can put your altar anywhere you want to, within the limits of your living conditions, and decorate it any way you want to. You can build a permanent altar on a chest or shelf or set up a temporary altar on the floor, in any room, even outdoors. All the books of instructions (including this one) set forth what the authors have learned about altars, what they believe, and what works for them — for like ritual itself, various arrangements and tools are commonly used. Some of these will be discussed in this chapter.

Most people who use altars end up creating their own unique altars; I've never seen two that look alike. Your altar is the place where you can unleash your creativity, where you can celebrate in visual, concrete form the grand diversity of the manifestation of the Goddess, where you can express all the shades and hues of your creativity ... and change that expression as often as you want to.

Nevertheless, as changeable as an altar can be, we need to learn what tradition says about ritual and altars so we have solid ground to build on. It's like the old story about Picasso:

before he turned to cubism, he had to learn how to draw people realistically.

So what does an altar look like? It can be anything from Spartan to baroque and beyond. As I have observed them, altars seem to be the place where it's not "less is more," but "too much is never enough." That is to say, your altar can be as simple as a blue birthday candle in a plastic holder next to a photo of your grandmother or an elaborate array of beeswax candles in bright holders among a fantastic collection of Goddess images, wands, feathers, tarot cards, jewelry and fetishes, and other symbolic goodies.

Here is an abbreviated description of the altar I had when I originally wrote this book. It was spread all over the top of my mother's cedar chest, and it was full, cluttered, and wonderful. I started with not one but two altar cloths, then put everything I could think of on top. The altar was set against a north wall (for grounding) in my home and I had several objects hanging above it, including pictures of goddesses. The following describes about half of the chaos-becoming-order that was my altar.

Across the back, left to right: a ceramic incense holder I made myself with a half-burnt smudge stick resting in it, sacred salt I mixed myself inside a ceramic sugar bowl my brother made 25 years ago, a 30-pound chunk of soapstone into which an owl is carved in bas relief, and a chunk of wood from a friend's tree. These last two were my major earth symbols.

In the next row: my athame; a glow-in-the-dark goddess, which I sculpt from acrylic clay and sell; my egg-shaped nest of wood spheres and a quartz crystal egg; a $3 gold-tone snake bracelet with red eyes; and a gold iridescent chalice full of beglittered wishbones; glass beads; and other treasures. In the next row: my two altar candles in holders with women's heads facing front and back (the two-way-looking goddess Cardea predated Janus); a glass bell with an elephant rampant and a beaded Goddess feather wand (these two were my major air symbols); my money jar and a tarot card; a big red crayon a friend gave me; one of the blue eversharp pencils I use to write rough drafts; and a chunk of raw carnelian (these three were my major fire symbols).

At the front of the altar were my water symbols: a Waterford chalice (Kildare pattern, Kildare being Brigit's home), a sand dollar a friend gave me, and two conch shells from another friend. On the floor on the front of the altar lay "Monty Python" (a stuffed snake my son got when he was five years old; I have since put antlers on it), and three small rainsticks. On the left side of the altar lay a blue basket for my candles and on the right side were my doumbeks and a little basket full of incense, oils, charcoal, and sand.

Whew!

You don't have to collect that much stuff. I'm obsessive and compulsive, and I use the excuse that I'm a writer on Goddess topics to acquire all these goodies. You don't have to be as cluttered as I am. But watch out. The Goddess and Her goodies will grab you.

But change comes even to Witches, of course, and a year after this book was first published I took that altar down and painted the cedar chest black. It's bare now. Today I have multiple altars. Against a north wall is one for Tara, groundedness, and manifestation. Green Tara is not strictly an earth goddess, but She helps keep me grounded and growing. Against an east wall is an altar for Brigit, creativity, and passion; against a south wall is the third altar, this one for Isis, love, spirit, and instinct; and against a west wall is the fourth altar, for Athene, intellectual endeavors, and fresh air. These are the four goddesses I love most and with whom I am best connected and work most often. It is my pleasure to honor them.

I have a hundred other goddesses and *chatchkes* among my

thousands of books and on most of the flat surfaces in my home, plus a portable altar for special purposes. I like to think I've simplified my life. If it doesn't sound that way to you, don't tell me.

All we really need for our altars, of course, are simple symbols for the four elements, a candle or two, and something to represent the Goddess (or a goddess).

All we *really* need is the Goddess. Her manifestation can be pure, invisible spirit.

Four Elements

The altar we create is an echo of Her continuing act of creation. We make our miniature universe—our altar—more concrete by placing symbolic objects on it. These symbols call forth the four elements and the four (or six or seven) directions.

I hope you spotted symbols for fire, water, air, and earth in the crowd of stuff on my old altar. Fire, water, air, and earth are the four traditional elements: they're the building blocks out of which all things, organic and inorganic, are composed. The idea of four elements, which have appeared in nearly all ancient and modern cultures around the world, was invented long before the atomic table, and elemental fire, water, air, and earth are not the same as literal, physical fire, water, air, and earth. In addition, some cultures have added other elements like wood and iron, and spirit is often considered to be the fifth element. That is, spirit is the *quintessence*, the sum of them all.

Of the four basic elements, fire and air are traditionally seen as projective and masculine energies, whereas water and earth are receptive and feminine energies. In the tarot, the two masculine elements are represented by phallic symbols (wands for fire and swords for air) and the feminine elements are a container (cups, for water) and a pentacle or disk (earth). Gold is also considered to be a symbol of the masculine elements, and its energy is projective, whereas silver is feminine and receptive. Many people thus wear their gold jewelry on their stronger hand (right if you're right-handed) and silver on the weaker.

The four elements make up not only the entire physical world but also human psychology, from the four "humours" of renaissance authors like Robert Burton and Ben Jonson to C.G. Jung's four categories and the temperament types listed in today's popular Meyers-Briggs personality inventory.

Because taxonomy is a human mania, people have been putting everything they can see, hear, feel, taste, smell, intuitively sense, or imagine into these four convenient pigeonholes: *everything* corresponds to elemental fire, elemental water, etc. Here are some common correspondences.[26]

Elemental Fire

Elemental fire rules hot places like deserts, volcanoes, bonfires, hearth fires, even our altar candles. It represents metaphorical heat, too: energy, creative "fire in the belly," will power, blood, and rising sap, as well as explosions and eruptions. In some traditions, elemental fire rules the south, noon, and summer; I see it as dawn and spring. Fire's colors are the reds and golds; its signs of the zodiac are Aries, Leo, and Sagittarius; its elemental spirits are the salamanders; its angel is Michael (pronounced "Mick-eye-el"). Fire's animals are dragons and lions, and its plants are the hot ones, like peppers, mustard, onion, and garlic, as well as red flowers. Goddesses of fire include Brigit, the hearth goddesses Hestia and Vesta, and volcano goddesses like Pele, Aetna, Fuji, and Iztaccihuatl. Fire's gods include Agni, Hephaestus, and Prometheus.

Elemental Water

Elemental water rules wet places like oceans and seas, the tides, rivers, springs, swamps, lakes, wells, and glaciers (which, since they're frozen, may also be ruled by earth). Elemental water rules the emotions and feelings, like love, sorrow, and courage, as well as intuition, instinct, and sensitivity. In some traditions, elemental water rules the west, twilight, and fall; I put water in the south and give it the flooding noon and summer. Water's colors are silver and all the hues and shades of blue and green; its signs of the zodiac are Cancer, Scorpio, and Pisces; its elemental spirits are the undines; its angel is Gabriel. Water's animals are the swimming ones—fish, sea mammals like dolphins and seals and whales, and sea birds. Its plants grow in the water—seaweeds, ferns, rushes, lotuses, and water lilies. Goddesses of water include the oldest ones: Isis, Tiamat, Yemaya, Mari, Atargatis, Aphrodite, Ix Chel, Miriam, and the Naiads and Nereids. Four watery gods are Poseidon and Neptune, Llyr and Osiris.

Elemental Air

Elemental air rules windy places like plains, hills, mountain peaks, and beaches above the waterline. Elemental air rules mental activity: intellect, knowledge, theory, and intuitive and psychic work, also letting go. In some traditions, elemental air rules the east, dawn, and the spring; I put air in the west, for dusk and fall. Air's colors are pale—white, yellow, blue-white; its signs of the zodiac are Gemini, Libra, and Aquarius; its elemental spirits are the sylphs; its angel is Raphael. Airy animals, of course, are the flying ones: birds and insects. Its plants are the ones that most often go into incense: frankincense and myrrh, also lavender, marjoram, mint, and sage, plus "air plants" that grow high up in trees, like bromeliads. Goddesses of air are the intellectual ones: Athena and the Muses, also Ninlil, Nut, Tatsuta-Hime, and Vajravaraki. Gods of air include Thoth, Enlil, and Mercury.

Elemental Earth

Elemental earth comprises the planet itself and all its earthy features: mud, mountains, caves, meadows and planted fields, and forests and groves. Rocks, crystals, metals, and bones are also ruled by elemental earth, plus earthworks like growth, sustenance, manifestation, abundance, material prosperity, birth, death, and silence. Nearly every tradition puts earth in the north, giving it rulership of midnight and winter. Earth's colors are greens, browns, and black; its signs of the zodiac are Taurus, Virgo, and Capricorn; its elemental spirits are the gnomes; its angel is Auriel. Earthy animals are snakes (which live in holes in the earth) and ruminants (cows, bison, deer, and others who graze), and earth's plants are grains, grasses, and root vegetables like potatoes. Goddesses of earth include Gaia Herself, Demeter, Persephone (as Queen of the Underworld as well as daughter and aspect of Demeter), Al-Lat, Ops, Frigg, Perchta, Hel, Tellus Mater, Nokomis, and the all-creating mother of Australia, Waramurungundji. Earthy gods are Pan and Cernunnos (the horny forest gods), Marduk, and most of the consorts who spend part of the year in the Underworld.

The preceding paragraphs are far from exhaustive. Please do research on your own for further additional correspondence to bring to your rituals.

There's a practical reason for knowing these elemental correspondences. Everything you add to your altar and your ritual reinforces your intention and pulls the specific elemental power into your mind and heart. Every correspondence touches your altered consciousness. The more you pile on, that is, the more you reinforce both your physical senses and your imagination, the better your magic will work. It's like vitamins, except that I don't think you can overdose on correspondences, at least not until you run out of room in your house.

For unencumbered ritual, you can use your common sense

and simplify things considerably. What do you associate with fire? Red and orange things, matches and candles, hot things. You could use a red chili pepper, an orange candle, even a kitchen match as your symbol of elemental fire. What do you associate with water? Water, fish, and other things found in water. Place a glass of water or a shell on your altar. What do you associate with air? Things that fly, like birds and bees. Place a feather or a butterfly on your altar for elemental air. What do you associate with earth? Rocks and plants. Use a quartz crystal point, a leaf, Indian corn or dried wheat, or a potted plant. What do you associate with spirit? Things invisible, or *all* things because the earth is spirit made solid. You can leave the center of your altar empty or put anything that appeals to you there, including a Goddess image. If you want to, you can redecorate your altar every day and use herbs for all four elements, or stones or pictures of goddesses or the four tarot aces.

Directions of the Elements

By now you're asking, which elemental symbol goes in which direction? That can be complicated, too, since the four elements are traditionally associated with the four directions, but different traditions have different arrangements. Here are the two most common arrangements.

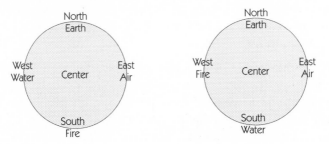

The first arrangement (on the left) is the most popular. It was invented in northern Europe, probably in the British Isles, and reflects the geography of the place. The North Pole is to the north, and cold = earth. The equator is to the south, and the hot climate = heat = fire. The Atlantic Ocean lies to the west, and trade winds (far to the south, to be sure) are easterly. The second arrangement (on the right) is based on Tantric tradition

My own preference is a third arrangement:

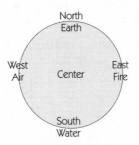

I noticed, years ago, that in the traditional arrangement the two masculine elements are adjacent to each other, as are the two feminine elements. This seems unbalanced, so I rearranged them to alternate the energies. Later, I met a professional astrologer who had come up with the same arrangement based on the cardinal signs (Aries, Cancer, Libra, Capricorn), which are traditionally associated with the directions as shown here.

I have also interviewed other people in other traditions, including a Native American shaman, and learned that they use still other arrangements, including two that put earth in the east.

You should use whatever arrangement feels most natural and works best for you, and you can create your own arrangement based on the geography where you live. Do you live along the East Coast? Water is to your east. Do you live in Illinois or Mississippi or Louisiana? If either of the first two, significant water (the Mississippi River) lies to your west; if in Louisiana, water can be either west or south (the Gulf of Mexico). Do you live in Iowa, Missouri, or Arkansas? If so, the Mississippi

River, your significant water, is to your east. Do you live within sight of a mountain chain? That's significant earth, whatever the direction. Do you live near Mount St. Helens or Kilauea? There are your fires.

The main things to keep in mind if you create your own arrangement are to *include all four elements* and, if you work with other people, be sure to discuss altar arrangements beforehand so everyone is in agreement and no elemental power is invoked twice or left out.

In my own work, more and more often, I invoke the elemental powers without reference to direction. The powers make up the whole universe, and I'm not sure anymore that they need to be associated with specific directions. The powers of the elements are *everywhere*.

Some people add two or three more directions: the center, plus up and down. The center is where the four quarters meet; this is the quintessential point, the direction of spirit. It's most common to put a goddess image in the center, but you can also use fresh flowers, a candle, or something that is special to you. I usually put something symbolic of my intention in the center, where it draws on the powers of the whole universe, that is, of the Goddess in *all* Her manifestations. The center is also where I put the candles or other things I use for the spell I'm working at the time. A peace candle is burning in the center of my altar as I write this.

Using up and down makes your circle a sphere, which is all-inclusive. Some traditions appear to use gods for up, presumably because air and fire rise, and goddesses for down, because water and earth are earthy. My preference is to visualize the four powers in three dimensions, which makes the center point an axis.

You can also see your sacred space as a spiral, or a point on a spiral, with all the women and men who worshipped the Goddess before you below you in the spiral and all those who will worship the Goddess in the future to come above you in the spiral.

If all this is too complicated to visualize, however, just see your sphere as a soap bubble in the sun and let the details fill in as they may. If you can't or don't want to see all this, all you have to do is believe it, at least during the ritual.

Finally, you can visualize your sacred space as the body of the Goddess. I was doing a 7:00 A.M. ritual before a cluttered altar with a friend one Christmas Eve, and suddenly I heard myself say, "The earth is our altar." I think that sums it up. The earth herself is our altar and we're part of the Goddess's ritual. As long as we state our intention and with words or without them invoke Her presence, the physical arrangements don't matter.

We should remember, also, that it's entirely possible to build a circle and an altar without any physical tools at all. We can do the whole thing in our imagination. I know a high priestess who does just that. When one of her apprentices is about ready for initiation, she sits down with him or her and watches while the apprentice casts a wholly mental circle.

Altar Tools

You may want magical tools. Like the altar itself, your tools can be elaborate and expensive or simple and unencumbered. You really don't need any tools except your imagination, but it's fun (and useful) to have them.

We don't really know much about prehistorical magical tools, partly because there probably wasn't a division between magical and "realistic." Every tool was a magical tool in the sense that its use added power to human labor. Hard, pointed stones were used to make other tools and carve sacred symbols into softer stone or pieces of bone or antler. Masks were worn in rituals in Old Europe, and numerous figures—nearly all of them female—have been found in sites in Europe and the Mid-East. Pottery was created to contain things. Ochre, an iron oxide found mingled with clay or sand, was ground up, mixed with liquid, and painted on corpses and in places like cave openings.

The so-called Witches of Medieval Europe were housewives and widows, so they used cooking pots, bowls, mortars and pestles, and kitchen knives and spoons as their magical tools. They probably couldn't afford candles, so they worked by sunlight, firelight, or rushlight. These women (and some men) were ordinary people who had learned a few things about herbs and healing and human psychology, and they worked with whatever they had at hand. They were also—during the years of the famous Renaissance of Cosimo de Medici and Leonardo da Vinci and during the Age of Enlightenment of Voltaire and the Royal Society—under threat of real danger, every day, from paranoid neighbors and the Inquisition. They didn't have altars, and they probably didn't even know they were "witches." They were just country people[27] whose neighbors turned to them and their "old religion" when they couldn't get the help they needed from the biophobic priests and doctors of the urban new religion.

The popularized rituals, altars, and tools we're familiar with today, therefore, aren't necessarily related to the ancient worship of the Great Goddess. They have been borrowed from ceremonial magic, a Judeo-Christian coinage which is itself a great borrower from the classical pagan cultures (mostly Egyptian and Greek), medieval Rosicrucianism, and alchemy.

Let's look at the four major ceremonial tools, which are the same as the four tarot suits: swords, wands, cups, and disks (or pentacles). They correspond (of course) to the four elements: swords = air, wands = fire, cups = water, and disks = earth.

Swords

I doubt that any woman ever accused of being a witch (except Joan of Arc) owned a sword. Kings, nobles, and warriors carried swords and were extremely jealous of their power. What women had were kitchen knives.

Today, instead of swords, some Witches own athames. The athame is a consecrated, black-handled knife that is used primarily to draw pentacles in the air. I also use my athame to dig old wax out of candleholders and slice apples; neither of these uses seems to have injured the dignity of the knife. I also know people whose athames are paring knives, Swiss army knives, large quartz crystal points, and crow feathers. But you really don't need a knife at all. You can use your forefinger to draw those pentacles during rituals.

Wands

The wand started out as a stick—a digging tool, the royal sceptre, a conductor's baton, the shepherd's crook and the bishop's crozier, the dowsing rod. In all cases, the wand conducts and directs energy. That is, it carries the energy in a specified direction. Hold and point your wand when you invite the elemental powers to your altar and your ritual. You can also use a feather, a quartz point, a flower or leafy branch, a stalk of dried wheat or other dried floral, or your fingers during rituals.

Cups

When cups become altar tools, they're called cauldrons or chalices. Both are symbols of containment and of the ever-nourishing, ever-productive womb and breast of the Goddess.

A big cauldron (which can be your Dutch oven or any other large pot from the kitchen) is appropriate for large outdoor rituals. Fill it about one-third full with sand or cat litter and burn incense (lots of it) for a really impressive effect. After you clean it out, you can also make soup or some other "witches brew." You can buy a small iron-footed cauldron at a gourmet or occult supply store and use it for burning incense at home.

Being a double Cancer, I'm attracted to water symbols and own over a dozen chalices, most of which began their lives as water goblets: my Waterford "Kildare" goblet, a couple of hand-blown glass goblets, a couple of silver ones, a couple of fancy ones from the local liquor store and a pricey department store. A Tupperware cup, while not as glamorous, would work as well, since the idea is more important than the form. If you're sensitive to smoke or don't want to set off your smoke alarm all the time (which is what happens when incense billows up), do your purifications with water in your chalice.

Pentacles

There seems to be some confusion about the difference between "pentacle" and "pentagram." The American Heritage Dictionary, for example, defines "pentacle" as "a five-pointed star formed by five straight lines connecting the vertices of a pentagon and enclosing another pentagon in the completed figure. Also called 'pentagram.'" I asked around for clarification and got two hints. First, the pentacle may be the star itself, which becomes a pentagram when it's encircled. Second, the pentagram is the geometric shape, whereas *the pentacle is the tool;* that is, the pentacle is the star carved on a wooden disk, painted on a plate, made into jewelry.

The pentacle was drawn by medieval occultists to protect themselves from the demons they conjured up. It also occurs in nature. If you slice an apple in half horizontally, for example, you see the pentacle formed by the seeds. The pentacle can be used as the earth symbol on your altar (use that apple you just cut open), and many Witches wear pentacles on chains around their necks. I don't, but I hang them in my home. I also have one tattooed on my ankle.

Making Your Own Tools

I prefer to make my own tools or embellish and personalize the ones I purchase. Sometimes I tie blue and silver ribbons around the stems of goblets, and I have decorated my sword (which I got when I was initiated into an occult order) with a big bouquet of ostrich plumes, ribbons, and bells. One of my friends used to balance it on her head when she was belly dancing.

If you want to make a wand, find a reasonably straight stick about as big around as your thumb and as long as your arm from your elbow to the tip of your index finger, though shorter is all right. Glue a quartz point on the smaller end (the end that pointed away from the tree) and wrap the stick with multi-colored yarn, embroidery floss, ribbons, or all of the above. You can use any colors you like, but remember that red and orange are the fiery colors. You can also add feathers, beads, shells, bells, seed pods, or any other decorations that appeal to you. When you do this, as explained in Chapter 2, you are practicing the presence of the Goddess and creating something precious; the creation is itself a ritual. If you make your own tools and symbols, they contain your personal energy, and that's what makes them truly magical. This chapter ends with a ritual to bless, or consecrate, your tools.

Costumes

There's a saying that witches are large women in colorful clothing. Maybe so.

Costuming (or robing) is an entirely individual matter: I think comfort is a major criterion, but others go for symbolism and style. In the privacy of your own home you can wear anything (or nothing), though it's good to keep something special aside that you wear only for rituals. Just as lighting your candles puts you into a magical mood, so does putting on special clothing. My preference is informal. I wear T-shirts about two sizes too large, with or without meaningful designs and slogans, and leggings. You can also wear a caftan that's roomy enough for you to sit cross-legged, an Indian cotton skirt, or a beautiful robe or peignoir.

When you go out to public rituals, it's fun to dress up. Laize Adzer's clothing (buy it at your local garment district) is ideal ritual costuming, as are Arabian dresses, Indian cotton skirts, and costumes whose elements you combine from many sources into a fantastic look.

Jewelry, both at home and in public, is also important. Some people wear every necklace they own, some wear outstanding earrings and bracelets, some wear only one special piece that they reserve for ritual work. I wear a necklace of Tibetan turquoise chunks and red coral to all rituals. Sometimes I also wear one of my glow-in-the-dark goddesses, which are about three inches tall, Neolithic-looking, and made of acrylic clay. If you play a hand drum, be sure not to wear any rings (they'll ruin the drumhead) or dangly, heavy bracelets.

Some of us also wear exotic scarves, body glitter, and wonderful feathered and sequined headpieces. Some of us are tattooed. Whatever you wear to a ritual, at home or in public—wear what makes you feel magical.

Candles

In addition to the traditional or nontraditional elemental symbols you place on your altar, you probably want at least one candle. Candlelight makes any occasion special, whether it's a nice soothing bath by candlelight, a candlelit dinner for two, or a ceremony of worship. Lighting a candle and extinguishing the electric lights signals a change of worlds; almost immediately the change of light casts you into a different mood.

You can use colored candles to enhance your intention. Although beeswax candles are more expensive than the tapers you can buy at the grocery store, they're worth the price. They smell good and burn clean, and hand-rolled beeswax candles are often made with oils or herbs and during the appropriate astrological sign to give you more correspondences for your ritual.

You can buy expensive, elegant candelabra, symbolic holders for single candles, or use the red clay saucers that you ordinarily set your flower pots in. This should be obvious, but I'll say it anyway: be sure your candle holders are fireproof; keep cats, ribbons, and other flammable things away from burning candles; and never leave burning candles unattended. If you're doing a seven-day spell, snuff or pinch the flame out each time you leave your altar and relight it when you return.

Here's something I do for many candle spells. First, I cut beeswax candles in half and put one or both halves on a brass or glass saucer. Under that, I put a wide, transparent plastic plant saucer, the kind you use to protect your tables. This is to catch any overflow of hot wax. Then I pour about a tablespoon of oil over the candles, something like Seven Powers oil or another intentional oil, though olive oil also increases the power of most spells. I also sprinkle appropriate herbs (mostly from my kitchen cabinet) on the candles. After I light the candles, I raise energy by chanting or drumming or listening to a tape, and I sit right there until the candles have burned down. With oiled half-candles, this takes about half an hour. After I've grounded the energy, I dispose of the wax, usually in the trash, though occasionally I'll bury it in the yard. Then I wash the candle holder so it's ready for next time.

Altar Etiquette

A note on altar etiquette: When you visit someone who has an altar or go to a public ritual, *don't touch the altar and pick up the altar tools or decorations without permission*. We charge our altars with energy for our intentions and build up our own energy in our tools. When someone picks up our athame or chalice, for example, it interferes with the energy and sometimes the charge has to be done all over again. This can be very annoying in the middle of a long-term spell; you have to begin all over again. Look at everything, therefore, and say "ooh" and "aah," but keep your hands in your pockets. When people come to visit you and look grabby, ask them firmly but politely not to touch, and explain why. If visitors won't understand, cover your altar before they arrive.

Porta-Witch

We don't do all our rituals at home. Like me, you may want to do a spontaneous full moon ritual on a hilltop or beside a stream. You may be asked to lead a ritual in someone's home or office. When that happens, you want to have your tools with you.

That's why I keep my Porta-Witch in my car. For years I used a plain cardboard box, but recently I purchased a covered basket in a thrift shop and decorated its lid. My new Porta-Witch contains the following objects:

1.   A compass. On the beach or in someone's living room, it's always important to know where the directions lie.
2.   Symbols of the elemental powers: a wooden egg with flames painted on it (fire), a shell and a 4-oz. silver chalice (water), three white feathers to which I tied tiny bells and crystal beads with blue thread (air), and a tiny silver lizard glued to a

rock glued to a stick (earth).

3. A miniature goddess or two.

4. Small plastic bags holding matches, self-igniting charcoal, sand, sacred salt, incenses, and oils.

5. Small red clay saucers to burn the incense in.

6 Four (unmatched) glass candleholders.

7. A ritual "knife" that is really a black letter opener with an owl handle and a "wand" that is really a sparkly silver pencil with a star over the eraser.

8. A generic altar cloth (a square yard of patterned cotton from the remnant counter).

9. Other treasures I have somehow accumulated.

The major problem with a Porta-Witch is candles: they melt together when you park your car in the sun. But that may be OK. It's safer, anyway, not to set fires in the woods — fireless altars can be perfectly beautiful — or other people can bring the candles. If a portable altar sounds useful to you, you can put together your own Porta-Witch.

A Ritual to Bless (Consecrate) Your Altar Tools

Traditionally, altar tools are consecrated to protect them from evil, or at least mundane, influences. Some tarot readers, for example, keep their cards wrapped in silk, and some people won't let anyone handle their crystals.

As I see it, respect is more important than protection. I keep my tools on or near my altar and handle them carefully. Unless they're just for decoration, I bless them to enliven them and give them a share of my personal power. Blessing your tools makes them more magical.

Fill your chalice about half-full with rainwater, spring water, or bottled water, and put a pinch of sea salt on a small saucer or a piece of white paper. Light either a white or a black candle.

Hold your chalice in both hands at your heart. Visualize a green light coming out of your heart, encircling the chalice, and infusing the water, then say these words:

> Powers of my love, powers of my life,
> Bless this chalice and the water in it.

Take a deep, strong breath. Hold it in your stomach for a few beats, then in your heart, then in your throat. Exhale strongly and slowly, seeing your breath as a gold and silver light. Let the light of your breath sprinkle into your chalice, infusing the water again.

> Powers of my life's breath and my soul,
> Powers of my inspiration and my expiration,
> Bless this chalice and the water in it.

Hold the pinch of sea salt in your stronger hand for a few seconds, then pour the salt into the water.

> As we were born from the sea,
> and saltwater is our blood,
> as it is the mysterious, holy blood of the Great Goddess,
> let this salt and water combine into inseparable strength.
> Let this saltwater bless and protect all it touches.

Set your chalice on your altar and pick up the tool you're blessing. If it's small, dip it in the chalice so it touches the saltwater; it it's too big to dunk, use your stronger forefinger to touch a few drops to the tool.

> Powers of the Great Goddess,
> Powers of water and earth,

Be present in my work,
Ensoul and empower my [tool].

Hold the tool near the candle flame (but not close enough to burn or scorch anything), then in the air above your head.

Powers of the Horned God,
Powers of fire and air,
Be present in my work,
Ensoul and empower my [tool].

Visualize the four elemental powers whirling around your tool, enveloping and penetrating it (they may look like colored lights). When it feels right to you, lay your tool on your altar.

After you have blessed as many tools as you want to, extinguish the candle and pour the saltwater on the earth (down a drain is permissible, but it's a poor second choice).

6

INVOKING
AND STIRRING UP
THE POWERS

When we invoke[28] (call in) powers, we may be addressing goddesses and gods and elemental spirits, but we're summoning our own inner power as well. All power exists both around us and inside us. Let's begin by examining invocations for extrinsic power, the transcendant powers of the universe, the invisible forces that we call goddesses, gods, devas, elemental spirits, angels, and so on.

Phrasing an Invocation

There are many ways to phrase an invocation. If you're in a real hurry, you can say, "Powers of Earth, be here now." Or "Yo, Mama! Come here to me!" These two, while direct, border on rudeness, however, and they're not very magical. The more poetical an invocation is, even if it's written or spoken in prose, the more magical it becomes.

In an invocation, we can use a traditional formula, like "Guardians of the Watchtowers, be present in our circle tonight and aid us in our magic." Another invocation I often use names many powers: "Powers of the North, goddesses and gods of elemental earth, gnomes, angels, winds, and devas, be present in our circle." Other variations include naming specific goddesses or gods. To invoke goddesses and gods of earth, for example, I might say, "Demeter, Cernunnos, and Auriel, guardians of elemental earth, we welcome you to our circle."

Another form of invocation is not to name a specific deity but to call forth the qualities of the elemental power and its direction, what I call the power's gifts. "Powers of the North, please be present. Come with your gifts of stability and abundance, darkness and manifestation to help us in our magic." The correspondences given in Chapter 5 provide abundant ideas for things you can say; it's even better if you use your own imagination and free association to call in what you want during a specific ritual.

Finally, you can describe the powers in a sort of prose poem:

Welcome, Powers of Fire, the element that burns. Fire can heat the air, scorch the earth, dry up water, and create drought, desert, and wasteland. But it also brings the warmth the seed needs for germination and growth. The powers of fire burn away the old and useless as well as things we think we still need. Fire is the power of passion and the clichéd "burning desire." It cauterizes wounds and gives us clean, fertile ground for new growth. Terrible and blessed are the powers of Fire.

Welcome, Powers of Water, the oldest element, the mother element, the most enduring of all the elemental powers. The races of all the children of Mother Nature, animal and human, were born from the sea, and each of us was borne in the sea of our mother's womb. We carry the waters of the sea in our blood. Where there is no water, there are aridity and death. Water's power is unutterably great. It carved the Grand Canyon, and floods and tidal waves can destroy whole cities. Nothing can halt the force of water. Seeking the path of least resistance, it flows around all obstacles and washes all things clean. Terrible and blessed are the powers of Water.

Welcome, Powers of Air, powers of the mind and the intellect. Air is the power of the breath that shows that a newborn baby is independently alive. It's the power of the winds that blow freely around our planet, across all lands and waters. The powers of the winds of change are in the air, the winds that blow away the old, useless things in our lives, sweeping us clean for new growth. It's the tornado and the zephyr. Terrible and blessed are the powers of Air.

Welcome, Powers of Earth, our Mother's body, our own beautiful bodies. Earth grounds and sustains us. Earth is rich with treasures and provides enough food for all her children. Earth is also the power of earthquakes, which destroy without discriminating between good or bad, rich or poor. And what is more powerful than an earthquake? A seed. Terrible and blessed are the powers of Earth.

Invoking a Power

A formal invocation commonly has four steps:

1. **Identify the goddess or god by name and attributes.** If you want to maintain any kind of control in your ritual, it's wise not to invoke anyone whose name you don't know—you never know who might show up if it's an open invitation, although these days it's highly unlikely that you'll attract anyone as wicked as Mephistopheles or Asmodeus (or even Cthulhu—and don't let fictions like "The Exorcist" scare you, either). The point is that it's more eloquent and gracious to invite deities by name.

And don't be afraid to invoke "found" goddesses. If you

look through books and lists and don't find a reference to a goddess who rules specifically what you want to do, *make one up*. A found goddess is one whose name no one else has found yet, though she's probably been there all the time. Found goddesses, being modern, are generally savvy as well as powerful, and they usually have a better sense of humor than the oldest goddesses, who have endured thousands of years of persecution and co-option.

For example, let's suppose that you live where I live, in Southern California, and we're enduring our fifth consecutive year of a drought. We want to do a rain ritual, using rain sticks and lots of blue candles, but we need a goddess of gentle rain, one who will revive our sandy soils without causing mudslides or floods. She'll be in the heritage of Tethys (mother of the Nereids) and Aphrodite, who was born in the sea, but not of Tiamat, who is too stormy. Perhaps she'll be related to the gentle Hesperides, who live and sing at the western edge of the world, for in the northern latitudes it's the westerlies that bring us the moisture-laden winds. We'll call her Mere (pronounced "Mare-ay"), a word related to both "mother" and "sea." One of the Virgin Mary's titles, in fact, is Stella Maris, "Star of the Sea." We can envision Mere as a mermaid. Our invocation begins:

> Hear us, gentle Mere,
> goddess of the sparkling sea,
> daughter of gentle waters, nourishing springs and tides—
> Watery Mere, hear our call....

2. **Flatter and praise the goddess.** Goddesses are as vain as we are, as you'll quickly learn when you read any mythology, and surely your grandmother taught you that we all respond more positively and quickly to sugar than to vinegar. Try this:

Beautiful Mere,
Crowned in pearls, robed in silver tides,
Gentle goddess
who brings soft rains and quenching waters
and shines in the rainbow ...

3.   **Summon the deity.** Invite her into your circle:

We call you to our circle, precious Mere.
Come into this sacred space....

4.   **State your petition.** Tell the goddess what specific kind of
help you want:

Gentle Mere, bringer of soft rains,
bring your gifts to our dried-out, thirsty land —
gentle rains, nourishing rains, soft rains
to satisfy our parched earth,
to revive our dying plants and trees
to let your children drink....

At the end of the ritual, thank the goddess and dismiss her. You
cannot, of course, really dismiss a goddess; she'll come or stay as
she wishes, but you can tell her your expectations:

Blessed Mere, rain gently on us
and then depart in peace with our thanks
and leave your rainbow as a sign
that when needed you will come again.

Having written our invocation to Mere, the goddess of gentle
rains, we're ready to do the ritual. We can play a tape of ocean
or rain sounds (but *not* one of the summer storm tapes), shake

rain sticks to raise energy, burn candles of watery colors (blues, aquas, blue-greens, silver), and put some real seawater in the chalice (the "seawater" can be bottled water plus sacred salt). To add one more correspondence we can do this ritual on a Monday, the day sacred to the moon that rules the tides and water, before noon to take advantage of the rising energy of the day, and during the waxing moon to use the moon's increasing power. I might also put my shiny pink beanbag mermaid on the altar and water all my houseplants right after we finish the ritual. All of these actions influence the powers of a benevolent, watery Goddess.

However we invoke the powers—wordlessly, briefly, or formally—we need to do something to raise the power we've invoked. Dance has long been a primary means to raise energy, and it is said that Shakti danced the universe into creation long before anyone made a statue of Shiva doing the dance. But when you're doing a ritual alone, you can't really do a complicated dance that requires partners. You can, however, put on a tape of lively music and improvise your own dance; or you can just sort of sway to the music and shake a rattle or beat a drum, or just clap your hands. The idea is to get the energy moving, and to do what you've got to do to get your own blood flowing energetically, in resonance with the rhythm of the invisible powers.

The energy is also part of you. You can see the "invisible" energy when you get centered. Here's what I do and what I experience. Your experience may be different in particulars, but in general, your experience should be similar to mine.

It helps to have outside stimulation—appropriate music, candlelight, a purring cat, an object of power like a wand or something else that ordinarily lives on your altar, even some everyday object like a rock. Everything pulses with energy all the time if you'll let yourself feel it.

At first I simply feel the energy. I feel my heart beating, my blood pulsing in my arteries. Then I begin to feel the energy around me. It's like gentle waves, or perhaps like being rocked in a cradle. Sometimes it's like I'm being stirred in the Crone's cauldron. The energy rises and circles, up and down, endlessly swaying and dancing, and I have to surrender to its motion. My breath always adjusts to this rhythm and I sigh a lot.

If I look with my inner eyes, I see sparkling black waves pulsing back and forth. Sometimes I see a silvery blue, and sometimes shoots of red and gold sparkles like dust motes in the sun. I also frequently see purple and green.

Sometimes it runs in patterns around me. The green helix I suggested in "A Ritual to Celebrate the Goddess in Women," at the end of Chapter 3, is typical. I also see ever-flooding pentacles, tracing and retracing themselves. I see rounded shapes with silver echoes and black velvet swirling in andante vortices. Sometimes I become very light-headed, sometimes I'm tingly, sometimes I get sleepy, sometimes I'm energized enough to work all night.

What I'm seeing and feeling, of course, is the activity of my own aura; what you're likely to see are the colors and special effects generated by your aura. But all the energy I experience is not intrinsic to me. I share it. My personal electromagnetic field is a part of the planet's electromagnetic field. This is how I know I'm part of the Goddess, how She is immanent in me, and why I love and worship Her as I do. We're all linked in Her consciousness and to Her dancing energy.

Seeing Energy

Try it yourself, with or without music, candles, or other props. Sit quietly, close your eyes, put your body and left brain in neutral, and wait. Pay attention to the beating of your heart and the suspiration of your lungs. Pay attention to the dances and flows inside your eyelids and around your body. That's genuine energy. It's always there. All you have to do is pay attention to it.

Pretty soon you can begin to nudge the energy, give it some direction, make it move around you. You can play in it as you did in the bathwater when you were four years old or as you romped in the Christmas Eve snowfall.

Now, if you open your eyes a bare crack, you may see the energy patterns. You'll recognize the energy as the same energies you see on sunny days when you sit or lie in the sun and open your eyes just a bit. When you can see the energy with your eyes wide open, you can begin to work with it.

It's comforting to see and use this energy. It's also inspiring, and people may begin to remark that you're more productive or creative. Other people will be aware of your energy, though they may use words like "charisma" or "motivation." They may tell each other that you're a "self-starter" or that you "can get the job done."

When you can see and feel the invisible energy without going into a trance, you can stir it up for ritual work and grab a handful or two for use in your everyday life. This isn't airy-fairy energy. It's entirely practical.

The next step is to direct the energy, to *use* that cone of power. You can guide it, mold it, form it, direct it. You can assert and express your will—state your intention—remembering, of course, that what you put out will come back at least threefold.

In ritual work, the energy is often shaped into a cone, which is sometimes called the cone of power. It has as many uses as you can think of intentions. When you're doing a solitary ritual, direct the energy in clockwise circles around your body and your space and start with the image of a bowl in your mind. You're stirring the energy up, and you want to keep it focused and not make a mess. Build up a cone that you can work with. It can be as gentle as a lover's touch, though it can also roar like a tornado. As you stir up the power, part of your job is to form it and not let it get away from you. Keep it under the speed limit, that is, until you're sure you can handle it without getting any celestial speeding tickets (which usually manifest as horrific headaches).

Don't try to show off, especially when you're working with a group. Get a fix on your own power and blend it into the group power. If you discover that you don't like the group power, you can always leave. The polite way to go is to draw a "door" with your fingers, wand, or athame in the boundary of the circle, go out, and close the door after you by drawing it in the opposite direction. If you're comfortable with the group power, add your power to it and follow the suggestions of the person leading the ritual. You can have some extraordinary experiences this way, and make interesting new friends, too.

Go back to Chapter 2 now and, knowing what you now know, begin again to practice the presence of the Goddess.

7

HOW TO TALK
TO A DEITY

Originally, when ritual was still part of everyday life and everybody talked to the Goddess, we spoke to Her in everyday words. As time went on and priests assumed more and more power, however, exalted language and fulsome invocations arose, and pretty soon only the High Priest could speak to the God Most High. That was the state of affairs for two or three millennia.

During the European Renaissance and all the way up to the 19th century Magical Revival, it was thought that all gods spoke Hebrew by choice, so Hebrew was the most common ritual language. Sometimes rituals were also conducted in Greek, Latin, crypto-Egyptian, quasi-Sanskrit, or Enochian (the "angelic language" of the Elizabethan Dr. Dee). If you read books on high occultism (try Israel Regardie's works on the Golden Dawn or the series by Denning and Phillips), you'll see scripts in these esoteric tongues. Trying to pronounce them can be like trying to unscrew the inscrutable.

Fortunately, someone discovered that it can be dangerous to invoke or evoke[29] an invisible power in a language you neither understand nor can enunciate precisely or improvise in. As anyone who has ever studied a foreign language remembers, boners come easily and can be very embarrassing. Worse, some powers get mad if you mispronounce their names, or you may not get who you intended to call. Like the modern Roman Catholic Church, therefore, occultists and others who do magic have generally adopted the vernacular.

But this leads us into a different verbal trap. Thanks to John Milton, John Bunyan, and James I of England (the king who authorized the 1611 Authorized Version of the Bible in English), most people seem to think that the divine eardrums resonate only to an approximation of Elizabethan English. Just eavesdrop on anyone offering a little prayer at the Rotary or Congress or a football game. It's really religiobabble: "thou art," "we beseech thee," "thou saidst," and so on.

Pagans do it too. I once attended a sabbat of perfectly normal Southern Californians that suddenly turned into a low-level Shakespearean road company.

If you really want to essay Elizabethan English to add a fancy touch to your rituals, follow these guidelines:

• "Thou" is the singular, intimate form of "you," like the French *tu* and the German *du*. Use "thou" to address *one* person or deity. Use "you" for *more than one*. Don't mix "thou" and "you" when referring to the same person.

Example: At the sabbat mentioned above, the circle was cast by each person anointing the next person with symbols of the four elements and saying, "*Thou* art god/goddess. I bless the divine in *you*." Wrong! It should have been "I bless the divine in *thee*."

• For the subject of a verb, use "thou." For the object of a verb or preposition, use "thee."

Examples:

> *Thou* art divine.
>
> I give *thee* my love.
>
> I bow to *thee*.
>
> I receive this gift from *thee*.

• The adjective form is "thy." If the next word starts with a vowel sound, use "thine."

Examples:

> *Thy* will be done.
>
> *Thine ea*rth is holy.

• Use the right number (singular or plural) of verbs:

Present tense:	I am	we are
	thou art	you are
	he/she/it is	they are
Past tense:	I was	we were
	thou wert	you were
	he/she/it was	they were
Future tense:	I shall	we shall
	thou shalt	you will
	he/she/it will	they will

• For other verbs and poetical constructions, get out your old copy of *Paradise Lost* and see how Milton, arguably the finest poet of the English language, said it. Or reread your favorite Shakespearean plays or sonnets. Keep in mind, however, that no one has spoken much Elizabethan English since the early seventeenth century.

Better yet, give the Goddess and the invisible powers some credit for keeping up with the times. In public or group rituals, speak to them in standard English or whatever the rest of your group speaks. And when you're not concentrating on getting archaic subject-verb agreement straight, you can concentrate on your intention and your visualizations.

You will notice that the rituals in this book are written in free verse (the Beltane ritual is a double sonnet). My reason for using verse is that verse is generally considered to be more elevated than prose. Verse (rhymed or unrhymed) is also easier to remember because of its patterns and repetitions, which also make the effect of the words cumulative. That is, they build to a natural climax.

When you create your rituals, however, you can use either verse or prose. Prose can be very poetic. If you do choose prose, your major concern should be controlling sentence length. You need to be able to breathe regularly. Long sentences leave anyone except a trained actor breathless, and we tend to stumble on the thorns of syntax when we go on and on and on. The best way to check yourself is to *read it aloud* and notice where you stumble, where your tongue trips over awkward clumps of consonants. That's where you rewrite.

You will probably notice the apparent simple-mindedness of the verses in my rituals, especially the love and money spells in Chapter 9. There's a good reason for simple-minded verse: it sticks in the mind and goes round and round. When you create your own verses, therefore, keep a few guidelines in mind:

• Choose a simple rhyme-scheme. AABB and ABAB are most common.

• Use simple words, words you understand, plain and direct words. The idea is to be direct and clear, not cryptic and clever. If you use rhyme, remember that you're not Stephen Sondheim, though by listening to his songs you can pick up interesting ideas about what can rhyme with what.

• Use a simple rhythm. Spoken English is very nearly iambic: di-DAH, di-DAH, di-DAH. Trochaic meter reverses the iambs: DAH-di, DAH-di, DAH-di. The other two common meters are anapestic (di-di-DAH, di-di-DAH) and dactylic (DAH-di-di, DAH-di-di). Shakespeare and Milton worked wonders with these four common meters; so have Dr. Suess and Paul Simon. So can you.

• Write in short lines of two, three, or four feet. Short lines put more energy into your ritual and are easier to remember than very long lines.

A Ritual to Honor the Goddess Gotcha

Does your life seem to be a play by Eugene Ionesco, with sets by Salvador Dali and music and lyrics by the Bobs? Is it *just too weird?*

I wrote this ritual the week my car was stolen the second time (but returned with all the contents intact, thanks to spells by my friends Marsha and Clarissa), my checkbook was acting like bad plumbing, I twisted my ankle at an earth renewal ceremony in which even the shaman himself got mixed up, and I finally admitted that, yes, I am addicted to Cheetos. Sometimes the world is an absurdist play.

Gotcha is the goddess of absurdity. Cognitive dissonance, practical jokes, and chaos are her realm, and she always wades in hip deep. Chaos science is a new way to explain the happenings of the world, and it's also a very old way. It's the mixed-up mixture of raw elements that churns in the cauldron of the Great Goddess, the randomness factor in the web of being. It's the absurd meaningless state that Samuel Beckett wrote about and that we see on the six o'clock news every night. (Supply your own examples.) It's characterized by the bumpersticker that proclaims "Shit Happens."

Chaos makes people nervous. We're not supposed to be able to live in it. We've been taught to crave order: files in alphabetical order, organized closets, pigeonholes for stamps and paperclips, school desks and parades in rank and file. It's a very left-brained world, indeed. There's a place for everything, and everything is expected to be in its place.

Or so we believe. But Murphy's Law kicks in on any given project. There are sudden mutations in diseases and insects. Earthquakes and drunken drivers change lives. Serendipitous meetings happen with significant people. Vivid dreams solve waking problems, an insight—aha!—unlocks an enigma, an absurd image answers the Zen koan.

In fact, we need a bit of chaos in our lives. Without it, we become too comfortable, which makes us lazy and self-satisfied. Without chaos, we might never get our act in gear. The intention of this ritual, therefore, is to recognize and honor the importance of chaos.

It's dedicated to Gotcha, who was in earlier times called Eris. You may remember Eris as the troublemaker who tossed the apple ("For the fairest") into the crowd at the wedding of Thetis and Peleus; selecting the "fairest" led to the Judgment of Paris, and Paris's decision led to the Trojan War. Eris was also the hag who wasn't invited to the christening of the princess but came anyway and delivered the pronouncement that turned the princess into Sleeping Beauty.

An appropriate time to do this ritual is during a void-of-course moon, which is when the moon has no aspects and no serious work can be successful.

Set up a chaotic altar. I set my stuffed Cheshire Cat doll in the center and add whatever I feel like tossing into Gotcha's chaotic cauldron. Skew the altar so nothing is where it's supposed to be. Make the axis northwest to southeast, for example, and move the directions and elements to random positions. If you have to, use Post-it™ notes to remind yourself of how you have arranged things. In my experience, the elemental powers don't seem to mind this disorderly arrangement. It gives them a new perspective on things and a bit of exercise as well. They also recognize the value and place of chaos in the created universe. After all, the universe was created out of chaos.

To cast the circle, begin with whatever element is at your right hand and move in a clockwise direction. Here's how I did it the other day. Adjust the directions and elements to your own (dis)order.

Powers of Earth, welcome to this circle of magical chaos and absurdity.

Found goddesses and mischievous spirits, you're the banana peel that makes us tumble head-over-heels, the crack on the sidewalk that pitches us on our ass.

Powers of chaos, I honor you today.

Powers of Fire, welcome to this circle of magical chaos and absurdity.

Found goddesses and mischievous spirits, you're the spinach in our teeth, the jelly donut on our tie, the fart and the belch in polite company.

Powers of chaos, I honor you today.

Powers of Air, welcome to this circle of magical chaos and absurdity.

Found goddesses and mischievous spirits, you're the run in our pantyhose, the open fly, the brain dump and the misplaced notecards.

Powers of chaos, I honor you today.

Powers of Water, welcome to this circle of magical chaos and absurdity.

Found goddesses and mischievous spirits, you're the joke we don't get and the blush when we do, the whoopee

cushion and the plastic dog turd, the mail addressed
to Occupant.
Powers of chaos, I honor you today.

Mighty and outta-sight Goddess Gotcha,
Eris, goddess of discord,
I recognize your actions in my life.
I honor your crucial role in creation, destruction, and re-
creation.
I know that where change is, there you are.
I welcome you and ask you to touch my life with giggles,
tomfoolery, vulgarity, and eventual understanding.
I seek the confusion I need to experience before I can sort
my values out and move into the next part of my life.

Mighty goddess, I whirl in your cauldron
I wait in your womb
I rise in your spring.
My intention is to question authority, examine all rules,
see through all pat solutions, and raise hell.
Hail, Gotcha, Fulla Fun and Outta Sight!

Sit quietly in the presence of the Goddess, thinking about your
life until you begin to laugh. Laugh as long as it takes.

PART THREE

TIME IN
THE GODDESS

TIME IN
THE GODDESS

Not only is the Goddess the mother of the cosmos and the earth embodied, as we saw in Chapter 3, but She's also time itself. She is, in fact, older than creation, because it was She who did the creating. The Goddess really is the Grandmother of God.

In addition, just as the Goddess contains all things, visible and invisible, in the cosmos and on earth, so is time the measure of all things. Only time—duration—measures the days of our lives, birth and death, growth and change, the turning and returning of the seasons. She is time in its unimaginable vastness, but She's also time in the utterly continuous re-creation of each instant, the rebirth that comes with every single heartbeat.

A number of goddesses, or manifestations of the Goddess, are in charge of time. The Greek Horae are the hours of the day and the seasons, which are the hours of the year. Elli, a Teutonic goddess of old age, wrestled the great Thor to the ground. At-En and Kali, Egyptian and Hindu, are dark, all-devouring goddesses; only time devours all things. Renpet, another Egyptian goddess, wears a calendar for a hat. The Fates and the Norns spin, measure, and cut the threads of our lives, and Unelanuhi is

the Cherokee "apportioner" who divides time into its con-
stituent units.

There are "patron goddesses" for nearly every day of the
year, and the pagan festivals celebrate these Goddesses. Many
of the old festivals survived as folk customs and superstitions
nearly up to the present day, and some of them are being
revived again by the earth-based religions. You can celebrate
today what the Mesopotamians, the Japanese, the Greeks and
the Romans, the Balts and the Celts, and the original Americans celebrated thousands of years ago.[30]

It's easy to observe for yourself how the Goddess embodies
time. Every day for a year, look at a tree. Don't make a big deal
of it, just look at the same tree for 365 consecutive days.

And every night, look at the moon. Between November and
February, you can usually see it as you drive home from work.
The rest of the year, look out your bedroom window, take an
evening stroll, go out and look at the moon during TV commer-
cials instead of scanning the contents of the refrigerator.

Watch a tree during the day, watch the moon at night, and
you'll see time happening. Since the Stone Age, the Goddess
has been the world tree and She's been the moon.

Look in the mirror.

Holidays of the Wheel of the Year

In Chapters 8 through 11, which carry us through time in the
Goddess, I briefly describe some festivals that have marked the
changes of the seasons for people all over the world, and I have
written new rituals and celebrations you can do by yourself or
with friends to observe the dancing of light and dark through
the year.

What we call the wheel of the year is said to have eight
spokes that signal the ancient, pagan, agrarian, and pastoral
festivals that told people when to plant and harvest and carry

out the other activities of their lives. As they're being revived today, the festivals are an amalgam of Greco-Roman and Celtic practices.

The quarter days are also called fire festivals because early peoples lit great bonfires to celebrate the light and movement of the sun and properly usher in spring, summer, fall, and winter. The cross-quarter days are the two solstices and the two equinoxes.

Both the year and the moon have eight phases during which light grows and declines and dark grows and declines:

Sun/Year	Moon/Month
•Candlemas, February 1	New Moon
•Spring Equinox, March 21*	First Quarter
•Beltane, May 1	Waxing (Gibbous) Crescent
•Summer Solstice, June 21*	Full Moon
•Lammas, August 1	Waning Crescent
•Fall Equinox, September 21*	Third Quarter
•Hallows, October 31	Dark Crescent
•Winter Solstice, December 21*	Dark Moon

To set out in time with the Goddess, therefore, we begin in the dawn of the year, at Candlemas, which is also the year's new moon. This is the season of quickening light, of waking up after winter's rest, it's the season of promise, potential, and laying plans and planting seeds.

We celebrate the growth of light and outward-bound energy through the spring and into Midsummer, which is the year's noon and full moon. This is the time when the seeds we planted in the spring bloom, when our days are warm and sunny. Potential becomes actual, it is the time of full power and manifestation.

With the summer solstice, which is the longest day of the

---

*These dates are approximate

year, comes the beginning of the growth of the dark, and we celebrate growing darkness through the fall. Fall is the season of harvests, of evaluation, of reaping what we sowed last spring. It's the season of quieter, inward-bound strength. Our days still seem long, but we also look forward to the longer nights of rest that the lengthening nights will bring. It's the time to come in and rest after our efforts, to do inside work, to relax in the beauty of the year's dusk.

As the wheel of the year makes its final turn, we enter the night and winter, which is the year's dark moon. This is the time to sleep and dream, to use the powerful inner energy the dark brings to do a final harvesting and examine the leavings of our year. And just as the summer solstice tips us over into the waxing dark, so the winter solstice tips us over again into the waxing light, and the wheel of the year becomes a spiral. It's the spiral of the days and years of our personal lives, the spiral of the eternal days and years of the Goddess. Sun, moon, time, us, the Goddess—we're all one, dancing on forever in resonance together.

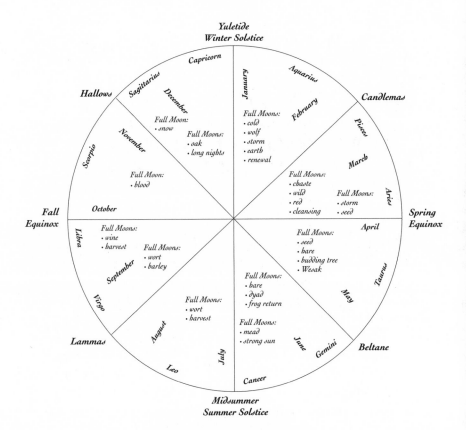

The Wheel of the Year

8

RITUALS FOR THE GROWING LIGHT: NEW MOON, CANDLEMAS, SPRING, BELTANE

The phases of the waxing moon grow in resonance with the brightening sunlight of the springtime. This is the time of beginnings and planting, and it's embodied in the Maiden, whose energy is potential becoming actual and whose traditional color is white.

You deserve a present for the new year; how about a lunar calendar? The one I use is created and published by Nancy Passmore.[31] Instead of laying the days and months out in rank and file like good workers on parade, the lunar calendar follows the spiraling dance of the moon from dark to bright and back to dark. It also gives times of the rising and setting of the sun, astrological transits (with explanations of what the transits mean), and special events like eclipses, and it's organized according to the magical Celtic tree-months, which are called "lunations."

As the owner of two small businesses, I hang my solar calendar (with Georgia O'Keeffe flowers) on one side of my office and carry an organizer with my dailies, monthlies, and yearlies all in a row; my lunar calendar hangs on the other side of my office.

New Moon Ritual: Planting Seeds and Wishes

The moon is new when you see the slimmest crescent outlining the right edge of the black disk, and we can generally do new moon work for two more days. New moon energy helps things grow, and when covens do new moon work, their intentions include getting things started, blessing and re-energizing ongoing projects, and healing. (You can, however, do healing rituals any time of the month.)

Taking the planting metaphor as my guide, I've created a new moon ritual you can use all year. Your first task every month is twofold: decide what you want and remember to do your own homework. (If you want thin thighs, one of my never-ending wishes, make a wish and then *exercise*.)

You need real seeds for this ritual—use any combination of sesame, poppy, or fennel seeds from your spice shelf, bird seed, a can of wildflower seeds, packets of flowers and vegetable seeds, acorns or other tree seeds. If you want to use specific seeds with specific correspondences, find the information you need in Scott Cunningham's *Encyclopedia of Magical Herbs*. Sesame seeds, for example, are ruled by elemental fire and the sun, which gives them projective energy; they are said to draw lust and money into your life.

Part of the ritual is heaping these seeds into a container that is meaningful to you, and since you'll be doing this ritual every month, you can use a variety of containers—your chalice, a special teacup, a measuring cup, a ceramic bowl, a red clay flower pot, a votive candleholder, the plastic egg your pantyhose came in.

Finally, you need one to three small pieces of clean white paper and a red pen or pencil (or crayon).

On the evening of the new moon, come to your sacred space, light at least one white candle, and invoke the powers of the elements and the Goddess, asking them to bless your beginnings.

Pour your seeds directly from your stronger hand into your container until it is nearly full, but not overflowing (so you won't have a mess of seeds to clean up).

Next, write your one, two, or three wishes (or one wish three times) in red ink on small pieces of white paper. Read each wish aloud three times (or one wish nine times), then roll each one into a tiny, tiny ball and bury it in your seeds. You can also bury a small crystal with your wishes.

Cradle your container in both hands and hold it at your navel. Read the following words, or tape them beforehand and listen to them, or use them as a model to make up your own words.

> Here I plant my dreams
> Here I set my wish —
> As I will it,
> let it be.
> Here I see new life
> Here I sprout new plans —
> As I will it,
> let it be.
> As I will it —
> growing, growing, growing.
> As I will it —
> budding, blooming, fruiting.
> As I will it,
> so must it be.

Sit quietly now, holding your seeds and wishes, and visualize how each seed between your hands holds potential life. Imagine these seeds splitting open, and remember that splitting open for new life can be uncomfortable. See your seeds sending roots down into the dark, nourishing earth and sending shoots up into the warm sunlight. Remember that a plant's roots are often as full and widespread as its trunk or stem and branches: there's as much below as there is above. Visualize your seeds living in the nourishing earth, seeking water, rising into the air, reaching toward the fiery sun. See your projects growing with these seeds, being nourished, blessed, and protected by the elemental powers of the Goddess, and know that new life will begin.

When you're ready, open your eyes, open your circle by thanking the Goddess and the elemental powers, and snuff out your candle. Leave the container of seeds on your altar or on a safe windowsill in the light of the new moon all night, and in the morning either plant them in your garden or elsewhere or toss them to the neighborhood birds.

During the month, take an active part to make your wishes take root and come to life. (You may find yourself getting synchronistic help.)

Candlemas Celebration: Self-Initiation
February 1-2

Candlemas, the year's new moon, celebrates the stirring of life and light after the long, cold winter's dark. Other names for this festival, which like all pagan festivals really begins at sunset, are Imbolc, Oimelc, Brigid's Day, and Groundhog Day. "Imbolc" is a Celtic word that refers to Mother Earth's belly or womb, where the year is quickening, and "Oimelc" refers to sheep's milk, "the ewes are pregnant." Brigid is St. Brigit, who first was the Celtic triple goddess Brigit. She is the goddess of fire and inspiration, poetry, smithcraft and other crafts, and healing. For this reason, you can also start, bless, and inspire new projects at Candlemas and do the new moon seed ritual, laying your chalice full of seeds right on the project or a symbol of it. When the groundhog comes out of his hole after his winter's hibernation, he looks around for sunlight; we, too, emerge from our own kinds of hibernation and look for the light. If we see our shadow, however, perhaps we should examine and confront it and find out what's holding us back. February 1-2 is the night when the Crone dies as all things must and the morning when she is reborn as the Maiden as all things are. In southerly latitudes, early planting begins; in more northerly latitudes, we set our seeds indoors with plans to transplant them outdoors when it's warmer, and we notice the early crocuses and violets in sheltered places outdoors.

Within a month of Candlemas, before and after, are national holidays that commemorate the groundbreaking works of great men—King, Lincoln, Washington—and the unobserved birthday of another groundbreaker, Susan B. Anthony (born February 14, 1820). Valentine's Day, of course, means flowers, flowering love, and a visit from the goddess Chocolata. The Chinese New Year is the second new moon after the winter solstice.

Initiation really signifies *a beginning* and, for this reason, many traditions initiate new witches on Candlemas after the traditional study period of a year and a day. I feel, as many people do, that self-initiation is the most effective, and initiation by another person is merely an outer echo of inner work. For this reason, I've chosen Candlemas to create a ritual celebration of self-initiation.

If you can, fast or at least eat only vegetables and drink only water on February 1. Set aside a couple of hours after sunset for your ritual and begin with a cleansing bath. After your bath, dress in loose, comfortable clothing that includes at least one black garment, like a shirt or a scarf around your shoulders. Have something white nearby that you can change into easily.

Since the true initiation is conferred by our inner self after we've made friends with our personal winter shadow and decided to live a new way, it's a *mystery*. What is mystery in this sense? It's something that cannot be spoken; it can't be spoken or documented because it simply can't be put into words. I can't (and wouldn't) initiate you into the practice of the presence of the Goddess, but if you're willing to do so, you can do it yourself. You're going to create your own mystery. Before you begin, ask yourself, what does your intention to practice the presence of the Goddess really mean to you?

If you already have or want to use an altar, set it up with your elemental symbols and a small black candle in the center. Half-way through the ritual, you will replace the black candle with one or more white candles (as many as you want), so leave room for them inside the circle of the elements. You can also place any symbol of the Goddess on your altar, either in the east or next to the center candle. Fill your chalice with water.

Wearing your black garment or scarf and burning your small black candle, you represent the Crone, the wise old one. This is the "old you" in several senses of the word. It's your chronological age (whatever it is, you're older than some of your friends). It's you before you're "reborn" as the Maiden. It's your past, all the things that have happened to teach you interesting lessons and bring you to the present. It's the old-fashioned you, the opinions and prejudices and outmoded ways of thinking that you can now discard.

Make the room as dark as possible. Light your black candle, then turn off all electric lights. Sit comfortably and cast your circle, invoking the elemental powers and the Crone (whose name is Hecate, Kali, Sarah, Baba Yaga, Befana, Sedna, or Weisse Frauen). Ask Her to bless and protect you in your new life. Establish a spiral of deep purple energy around your body, and when you're ready, read the following words or tape them beforehand and listen to them or use them as a model to make up your own words.

I am the old one
I am the old year
I am the wise one
I am the dark one.

I have been asleep
I have been failing
I have been out of date
I have been dreaming.

Close your eyes and sit in your purple circle as long as you want to. Observe the energies around you, watch the movies inside your eyelids, follow the paths of your thoughts. Consider where you have been in this life and where you wish to go.

When your own "small, still voice" tells you it's time, open your eyes. Take a sip of water and use your fingertips to touch a few drops of water from the chalice to the top of your head, your forehead and eyes, your throat, your heart, your navel, your sex, and your hands and feet. Light your white candle from the black candle and snuff out the black candle. If you have more white candles, light them from the flame of the first one. Set the extinguished black candle behind you. Take off your black garment and put on your white one, then read these words:

I see the new light
I see the shining one
I see what lies ahead
I see the young one.
I am the light one
I am the fresh one
I am the new year
I am the new one.

Close your eyes again and see the spiral of purple energy become white. You may want to chant or sing Goddess songs for a while, or you may just want to sit in silence again.

When you're ready, open your eyes, drink the rest of the water, open your circle, and extinguish the candles. Whatever has happened—and it may seem as if nothing has happened—is what was supposed to happen. Even though its effects may not manifest in your everyday life for some time, you have indeed initiated yourself.

Spend the next day in celebration. Wear white clothes if you can and spend time with new friends as well as old ones.

Spring Celebration: An Earth Day
March 20-23

At the spring equinox (check your calendar for the exact date), dark and light are in balance. Night and day are of equal length as the planet crosses the celestial equator.

Other names for the first day of spring (and Aries) are the vernal equinox, Oestre, Ostara, and Eostar. Easter and Passover (Pesach) also fall close to the spring equinox. Easter, one of the Christian Church's "moveable feasts," is calculated to fall on the first Sunday after the first full moon after the equinox. Passover begins on the 14th of Nisan, which is the month of the lunisolar Hebrew calendar that falls in March or April.

Oestre, Ostara, and Eostar are northern European names for Astarte, who is also Ishtar and Astoreth. Astarte means "womb"; at this time the Goddess as the earth is pregnant, and plants and animals are being born all over the planet. As the goddess of the morning and evening star, Astarte is also Venus, goddess of love, passion, and creativity. In the story of Demeter and Persephone, this is the time of Persephone's reappearance on earth. The awesome Queen of the Underworld becomes her mother's daughter again, and Demeter permits vegetation to ife.

⹀ feast of Esther, the Hebrew queen who saved the Jews of Persia, falls around March 24. As her name reveals, Esther is also Ishtar and Oestre, and both her name and story come from the story of Ishtar and Marduk (Mordecai). In England, March 25 is Lady Day, celebrating the Annunciation of the Virgin Mary, whose iconography echoes that of Isis.

The spring equinox also marks the sacrifice and resurrection of the consort/son/sun gods: Adonis, Attis, Dumuzi, Jesus, Mithra, Osiris, Tammuz, and Vishnu, among others. Most of these gods were born to virgin mothers at the winter solstice, most of them are teachers of the living or judges of the dead, and most of them spend a symbolic period of time in the Underworld before they rise again. None of them ever really dies, although their apparent deaths are mourned vociferously. St. Patrick's Day is likewise celebrated in March. He probably didn't even exist; his "autobiography" didn't appear until 400 years after he died, and the "snakes" he drove out of snakeless Ireland were pagan priestesses, the snake being an ancient symbol of regeneration and the Goddess.

Following my own informed intuition rather than any particular tradition or teaching, I choose the spring equinox to celebrate the earth and honor Mother Nature. Let's make today our own "earth day"!

Even if, like me, you'd rather enjoy the great outdoors through a window, this is the day to actually get out in it. Practice the presence of the goddess of creation and destruction in her natural home as much as you're able. Even if it's a regular workday, get outside for a few minutes early in the morning. This is a good day to take a closer look at your tree. At lunch, take a walk to the closest park or at least visit a garden shop or a florist. When you can, at work, chat with your associates about environmental issues as they affect your lives.

When you get home, spend some time picking up trash on your property, around your apartment or condo, even on the little patch of sidewalk outside your front door. If you haven't done so already, set up a home recycling center; at the very least, you can use empty brown paper bags from the grocery store to hold old newspapers, aluminum cans, plastics, glass, and real trash.

If you can, do your spring ritual on the rising tide of the equinox. The rising tide is the ideal time to do any ritual, for when the energy is rising, it's stronger. You can get exact hours of equinoxes and solstices and full moons from your lunar calendar. Adjust for local time and daylight savings time, then plan your ritual for shortly before the actual equinox. This is the ideal; if this timing won't work, however, don't worry about it. The Goddess certainly won't. Do your ritual at the nearest convenient time.

Use spring-colored candles for your spring ritual—as many candles as you want in aquas, pinks, yellows, pale greens, violets—and wear spring clothes, maybe even a flowery hat. Decorate your altar and your home with fresh flowers, colored eggs, and anything else that means spring to you. If you can find an outdoor space that's safe from prying eyes and fire hazards, do the ritual there. Under a big friendly tree and beside a sparkling brook is ideal; lacking these, find a friendly twig or a leaf and put some spring water or rainwater in your chalice.

For your elemental symbols, use your wand or a red candle for fire, your chalice or shells for water, feathers or butterflies for air, and a living potted plant for earth. For your Goddess symbol, find an earth. It can be your childhood school globe; an inflatable or stuffed, huggable earth; or the sphere from your nested set that represents the earth. Whatever you use, it should be a planet you can hold in your hands.

Cast your circle as follows, remembering that my preference is fire/east, water/south, air/west, and earth/north. If you prefer a different arrangement, adjust the verses of the invocation.

Touch your wand or candle (unlit) to the little earth on your altar.

> Gentle Pele, Goddess of Fire,
> Flaming Elemental Powers who dwell
> in bonfires, volcanoes, and deserts—
> join my circle
> and bring your gifts:
> golden energy to warm Her
> purifying flames for new growth.
> Fiery Powers of the Goddess,
> help me heal the earth.

Lay the wand or candle back on the eastern side of your altar and light the candle. Touch your chalice or shell to the globe.

> Gentle Yemaya, Goddess of Oceans,
> Watery Elemental Powers who dwell
> in oceans, rivers, and springs—
> join my circle
> and bring your gifts:
> blue energy to bathe Her
> rushing tides to give Her courage.
> Watery Powers of the Goddess,
> help me heal the earth.

Lay your chalice or shell back on the southern side of your altar. Touch the feathers to the globe.

> Gentle Tatsuta-Hime, Goddess of Air,

Soaring Elemental Powers who dwell
on hills, plains, and mountain peaks —
join my circle
and bring your gifts:
silver breezes to cool Her
roaring winds to scour Her clean.
Airy Powers of the Goddess,
help me heal the earth.

Lay the feathers back on the western side of your altar. Touch the potted plant to the globe.

Gentle Nokomis, Goddess of Earth,
Grounded Elemental Powers who dwell
in caves, forests, and groves —
join my circle
and bring your gifts:
green growth to nourish Her
darkness to enrich Her.
Earthy Powers of the Goddess,
help me heal the earth.

Lay the potted plant back on the northern side of your altar. Hold your globe in both hands at your heart.

Great Goddess of the Plants and Animals,
You create all, You destroy all
And You bring all things forth again to new life.
Holy Goddess, Mother Earth,
teach me to honor You
teach me to protect You
teach me to preserve You.
As You will it,

so shall it be in me.

Lay your earth back in the center of your altar and close your eyes. If you have a rattle or drum, begin a heartbeat rhythm and make it louder and faster as you visualize all the colors of the rainbow rising from the little earth on your altar. Watch the energy begin to spin around the globe, around your elemental symbols, around your altar, around your home. Direct this energy through your community, your city and state, and watch the power touch places that are endangered by pollution or overdevelopment. Finally, direct the energy around the planet and see it shining upon and through our little blue planet moving in black space. Sustain this vision as long as you can, then release it by shouting or whispering, "So mote it be."

Ground yourself and open your circle.

Beltane Celebration: Passion
May 1-2

The light's getting brighter, the days are getting longer and warmer, and we know that spring is melting into summer. There's more life blooming and buzzing around us than we remember from last year, and May is bustin' out all over. It's Beltane, May Eve, Walpurgis Night, the festivals of Floralia and the Bona Dea. It's Mother's Day. It's the season of the Maypole and May baskets, the night of the sacred marriage (*hieros gamos*) between the May King and the May Queen. It's the night for making whoopee.

The "Bel" in Beltane may be a Celtic word meaning "bright," or it may be a Northern version of Baal, the Canaanite word that means "lord." "Tane" comes from the Celtic word *teinne*, "fire." Baal is Astarte's consort, and the title was also given to the human kings who performed the *hieros gamos* with the priestess who embodied the Goddess; this ritual mating legitimatized the king's right to the throne. Numerous myths (like the Arthurian stories) also show how the health of the kingdom reflects the personal health of the king, who originally, at least, ruled as the representative of the Goddess. The fertility and procreation of the king/god and queen/goddess were also reflected in the land, crops, animals, and people.

In the olden days in northern Europe, all four of the major pagan festivals were celebrated with bonfires that symbolized the heat and fertility of the sun and the sun gods. These fires had both practical uses—cooking the feasts, providing light and warmth—and magical uses—blessing, healing, disease prevention, and fertility.

Astarte in her many names was traditionally represented by a tree, as, for example, the *asherim,* or groves of Asherah, that were forever being condemned and chopped down by Jehovah's misogynistic prophets. The specific tree associated with Beltane is, of course, the Maypole, around which men and women dance a spiral dance and wind ribbons until the pole is bound up (and the men and women are *very* close together).

Symbols are usually complex and contradictory, however, and so the Maypole is also a phallic symbol. In fact, the original Maypoles may have been erect phalluses. The Maypole set into the earth in the middle of a grove, therefore, represents the *hieros gamos,* and I suspect that the spiral dance and the ribbons thus became a kind of elaborate foreplay. Perhaps we should also take note that the other popular symbol of May Day, the flower-filled May Basket, is a container. It's a symbolic womb.

It's Beltane, and we simply cannot escape the symbol and the act of love. Our Beltane ritual celebrates passion.

This Beltane ritual is a very private one best done in the bedroom unless you know a very sacred and secluded space outdoors. If you're part of a heterosexual couple, you already know where your Maypole and May Basket are. If you're part of a homosexual couple, you also no doubt already have a living or artificial Maypole, and if you're currently unpartnered, you may also have a very special Maypole (one with a battery?) and be ready to celebrate with yourself. In this age of AIDS, please do *not* go out and get just any partner; the god and goddess, the May King and May Queen, live in each one of us.

Decorate your sacred space in hot colors, especially rose, and bring in flowers, ribbons, lace, bells, shells, perfumes, sweet-smelling incense, and as many bright candles as you want. Cast a large circle and use flowers for your elemental symbols. Carnation and marigold are ruled by fire, daisies and African violets by water, goldenrod and clover by air, and honeysuckle and tulip by earth. You can find other vegetal correspondences in Cunningham's *Encyclopedia of Magical Herbs* and decorate with fruits, herbs, vegetables, and trees (leaves) as well as flowers.

When your Maypole is erect, decorate it, too, and also be sure to decorate your May Basket. (Use your imagination.)

At Beltane we invoke the blessings of both the Goddess and Her Consort, the Horned God, whom I like to call the "horny forest god." Which partner invokes which deity in this ritual is your decision. You can also make up appropriate gestures and (inter)actions to go with the verses.

> I seek the May King
>> strolling in the woods
>> waiting under leafy branches
>> trailing vining love.

> I seek the May Queen
>> dancing in the meadows
>> courting in the wreathing gardens
>> drawn by gentle doves.

I seek the Lord of blazing light
    rising golden sun
    passion's fragrant touch
    early morning, brilliant noon.

I seek the golden glowing Lady
    shining in my hands
    warming all she touches
    crystal day and ardent moon.

I seek the Beltane lover
    antlered god of plenty
    passion's treasured beast
    thrusting, plowing power.

I seek the Beltane lodestar
    goddess of the hornèd moon
    fallow field abiding
    fertile mother, sacred bower.

I am the Lord of passion, light, and fire,
I, the mighty one, greening all the earth.

I am the Queen of passion's sweet desire,
I, the generous one, giving all things birth.

Do what comes naturally to raise power together, and when
your Beltane celebration is quiet again, open your circle and
give thanks.

9

RITUALS FOR
THE BRIGHT LIGHT:
FULL MOON, MIDSUMMER

In the monthly cycle, we see the brightest light at the full
moon; in the yearly cycle, we see it at Midsummer. The
bright light brings growth and manifestation, it makes leaves
manufacture chlorophyll and flowers bloom, it brings people
out to parks and beaches for picnics and games. The full moon
represents the Mother aspect of the Triple Goddess, and its
color is red—the red of her blood and ours, of the root chakra,
of robust flowers. The summer solstice is the longest day and
shortest night of the year, and many of us find ourselves having
short nights as well during the full moon because the energy's so
intense it keeps us awake. In fact, because the moon is so big in
relation to the planet, and so close, it has twice the tidal tug of
the sun. We're flooded with the energy of the full moon and the
solstice, and all kinds of interesting things rush into our lives.

Full Moon Ritual: Drawing Down the Moon

All the full moons have their own names—long night moon, wolf
moon, chaste moon, seed moon, harvest moon, blood moon, etc.
(see page 135) based on their seasons. There's also the blue

moon, which occurs about every 33 months when there are two full moons during one calendar month. I created the full moon ritual given below on the night of the blue moon of December 31, 1990.

Full moon lore is recognized around the world, by peasants and scientists, urban professionals and pagans alike. The full moon pulls up the highest tides in the oceans, in "solid" land, even in the atmosphere. It makes people and other animals feel sexier, and reports have shown that more babies are both conceived and born at the full moon than in other phases. It makes us make both love and war, however, for nearly any cop or other emergency worker can tell stories of how the "crazies" and the "loonies" come out and commit weird crimes. The full moon even brings out werewolves.

We who work with the Goddess work on earth with the energy of the moon. Covens ordinarily meet every full moon (this meeting is called an esbat) to do magical work and worship.

In traditions closer than I care to be to ceremonial magic— traditions in which people work in pairs and covens are led by a High Priestess and (preferably) her mate, the High Priest—a major element of casting the circle is drawing down the moon. The High Priestess stands with her back to the altar, facing the coveners, and the High Priest gives her the traditional Fivefold Kiss along with a poetical blessing during which he invokes the full moon as Mighty Mother, Bringer of Fruitfulness. The High Priestess draws an invoking pentagram in the air, pulls the energy down through her body into the circle, and recites the Charge of the Goddess (which you can find in several books and the Motherpeace Tarot deck).

When we do unencumbered rituals alone in our bedroom or living room, we want something simpler. We're drawing Mother Moon's energy down into our bodies for healing, into our lives for success or prosperity (of many kinds), or generally into the world instead of into a specific coven.

You can do this ritual during the two days before the moon reaches fullness (when the energy is building). It's best done at night when you can see the moon shining through your window. Before you begin, go outside and actually look at the moon. Unless it's freezing cold or pouring rain, spend at least five minutes letting the light of the full moon shine into your eyes. Breathe it into your heart.

Use either silver or red candles (as many as you want). Silver represents the full moon, red represents the Mother: full power, full fertility, full manifestation, full light. Sit comfortably in front of your altar. If you're drawing the moon down into a project, have the project in your lap or on your altar; if it's too big for that, hold something that represents it.

Cast your circle and state your intention aloud. Ask the elemental powers of the Goddess for their help and blessings in manifesting energy into something solid and material.

This is a silent ritual, though you can play water music or other, more energetic music. I've also used a rattle to help build the energy.

Lay your hands flat, thumbs and forefingers touching to form a rounded diamond (or yoni), on whatever you're drawing the energy down into. Take several deep, easy breaths and close your eyes. Remember what the full moon looks like and visualize it above and slightly behind you, shining in full force on the top of your head and all the way down your spine.

See and feel the moon coming closer and closer to you until it touches you. The touch may be as gentle as a butterfly's wing or it may feel like a firecracker or a hammer. If it's too strong, breathe deep again and visualize some blueness in it for cooling. See and feel the full moon surround you, filling every atom of your body, flooding your circle and your altar. Don't rush this process. Pull the moon in slowly and really feel it. It's not make-believe; this is really happening. With each breath, pull more power into yourself, into your circle, into your project. I usually feel pressure at the top of my head, my shoulders begin to shake, I become tingly all over, and I feel so heavy I could almost sink into the earth.

When you feel that the full moon is present in your sacred space and you're present in the moon, pull the power through your arms and hands into whatever you're holding. If you're doing a healing, lay both hands where you need to be healed or lay one hand there and shake a rattle with the other. Do whatever occurs to you to pull the power through. You can also chant: WE ALL COME FROM THE GODDESS AND TO HER WE SHALL RETURN, LIKE A DROP OF WATER FLOWING TO THE OCEAN, or SHE CHANGES EVERYTHING SHE TOUCHES, EVERYTHING SHE TOUCHES, CHANGES.

Chant or sit quietly, feeling the power of the full moon flowing through you, as long as you want. Be fully aware that you are a channel for this energy, a conductor, a drainpipe, and that you're well insulated inside your circle. You can also let the energy flow out around you to share with your community.

When you're ready, release the energy. I usually do this by visualizing a giant soap bubble bursting in very slow motion.

Open your circle and ground yourself. If you need more grounding, eat something earthy (root vegetables, bread, crackers, etc.)

Other Rituals for Waxing Light: Love and Money

During the two weeks of waxing light from new moon to full, or on the full moon, you can do other rituals of increase. Since nearly everybody wants more love and more money in their lives, here's a ritual for each.

For a ritual to attract love in general or a special lover into your life, it's important to stimulate all your senses, to feel sensual, warm, and powerful. Sprinkle your altar (and yourself, if you feel like it) with dried rose petals and leftover Valentine glitter. Shiny red and gold hearts are fun. Burn rose or vanilla candles or potpourri. Have fresh strawberries, peaches, and apricots (fruits of love) ready to eat afterwards and cut an apple in half crosswise so you can see the pentacle its seeds make. Put daisies, bachelors buttons, sweet peas, and lilacs on your altar and all over the house. Wear pink and play soft, sweet, romantic music. Put lots of shells on your altar; conch and scallop (find pink ones) are traditionally associated with Aphrodite.

Find out which goddesses of love you want to invoke: Aphrodite, Venus, Oshun, Ishtar, Freya, Voluptas, Eurydice, Galatea, Psyche. There are goddesses of love from every country and era and for every aspect of love from the downright physical to the tenderly spiritual. You can even find your own goddess—how about Désirée or Moan Amour?

Open your circle by asking the elemental powers to bring the right person to you. But don't name a specific person; if you get what you ask for, that person could resent having been manipulated. He or she could also turn out to be a real jerk when the nimbus of infatuation and lust fades away.

Ask the Goddess to bring love to you. Address Her as Mama and really talk to Her. Tell Her how lonely you are, how much you want to share your life. Describe to Her what your ideal lover might look like, the qualities this person might have—kindness, respect, intelligence, sex appeal, playfulness, domestic talents, artistic talents, mechanical talents. Tell Mama all about the love you want and the lover who will bring it to you. Then tell Mama what you can give that lover. Be specific about all your good qualities, also what habits you know you need to change, and how you intend to change them. Tell Mama how loveable you are, how much you deserve to have love in your life. She already knows all this, of course, but you need to hear yourself saying it *aloud*. Really put some feeling into it, too. Become passionate!

Now take the apple you cut in half and hold a half in each hand with your arms outstretched. As you chant one or more of the following verses (and make up some verses of your own to add to the chant), bring the halves of the apple together as if in a loving embrace. It's OK if you make applesauce while you're doing this; your enthusiasm proves your conviction.

> Aphrodite, Cupid, Psyche —
> Bring my lover swiftly to me.

> Freya, Oshun, Venus —
> Nothing comes between us.

> Anahita, Deirdre, Ishtar —
> Bring my love from near or far.

Chant these little verses over and over again as you visualize your lover and raise your cone of power. When it's time, send the cone straight up and open it like an umbrella so it will sprinkle a loving glow down upon you wherever you go. Trust the Goddess to find you a loving person and bring him/her into your life. Be prepared, also, to take an active role; you can't realistically expect the person to just come knocking at your door (though it has been known to happen).

Now you have a choice. You can lay the two halves of the apple on opposite ends of your altar and do the ritual every night until the next full moon, moving the halves closer to each other each night. Begin this ritual at the new moon, so you're doing love rituals for two weeks. On the night of the full moon, reunite the apple, and the next morning throw it into running water or bury it with a final chant. Alternatively, you can eat the half in your stronger hand and lay the other half in the center of your altar. Cover it with sesame seeds, rose petals, lavender, or ginger (or all of the above). Repeat the chanting every night until the full moon, and then throw the apple into running water or bury it with a final chant.

Open your circle, give thanks, and ground yourself.

To attract abundance, material prosperity, and money into your life, surround yourself with green, silver, and gold or orange. Burn candles of these colors and dress in these colors.

You can make a money jar by filling a clean jar (a spice jar is about the right size) with silver coins (dimes), agates (especially moss agates and golden jasper), aventurines, allspice, pine needles, sesame seeds, rock salt, and fishhooks (to catch the wealth and hold it). Seal the lid of the jar with green wax and keep it on your altar next to your symbol of elemental earth or wherever you stack your monthly bills when they come in.

I use a special candle setup: three halves of beeswax candles set close together in a tight triangle on a brass saucer. Use two green and one orange or gold. Next, sprinkle a pinch each of sesame seeds, allspice, cloves, ginger, cinnamon, or all of the above over the candles, and then pour about a teaspoon of olive oil or "Nine Powers," "Seven Powers," or "Money Draw" oil over it all. (You can buy the last three oils at an occult supply shop.) This setup gets *very* messy when the candles burn, so put a bigger saucer underneath to catch the drips. The spices will make the candles burn fierce and fast, and it may even shoot off little sparks. The green, again, symbolizes elemental earth, and the spices are ruled by fire.

Cast your circle, asking the elemental powers for riches, wealth, prosperity, abundance, and good sense. Next, invoke a goddess of abundance: Juno Habundia, Ops, Ganga, Sarah,

Menrva. You can also find your own goddess — Goodie Getty or Susan B. Anthony, in whose honor a silver dollar was cast.

Now talk to Mama about what you need. Show Her all your bills and your battered checkbook. Explain to Her what your obligations are and how you intend to meet them. Tell Her how you'll cut all your credit cards in half and get a better job. Reassure Her that you won't just run out and spend this new wealth on clothes and ice cream and other stuff you don't need. Next, tell Mama that you deserve to be prosperous, and remind Her of the ways in which you're already rich — good health, loving family and friends, a good job or career, a few nice things around the house. She already knows all this, too, but you need to hear yourself saying it *aloud*. If necessary, keep saying it until you start to believe it.

To raise power, use a rattle or drum or clap your hands as you chant the verse over and over again. Visualize money, checks and dividends, and job offers (or whatever you asked for) pouring in to you and piling up around you.

> The things that I need,
> the people I've seen,
> the wealth I'm deserving —
> make everything green.
> Green money, green,
> bright silver and gold —
> come to me swiftly,
> come in from the cold.

Send your cone of power out to every source of income you can think of — companies that can hire you, clients who can engage your services, things you can sell, people who owe you money, grants, gifts, etc. See these sources returning the energy you're sending out, returning it in the form of checks, cash, whatever you need. Don't forget to consider barter as a form of energy exchange.

When you're ready, open your circle, give thanks, and ground yourself. Candles prepared as described burn down in about half an hour of nifty blazing and sparking.

Midsummer Celebration: Personal Power
June 20-23

Midsummer's Eve and Day (check your calendar for the exact dates) are the year's full moon. Other names for the summer solstice and first day of Cancer are Litha and St. John's Eve. Litha is the name of a northern European (or North African) goddess of fertility, power, and abundance; the pagan holiday was conflated with the birthday of John the Baptist (traditionally June 24) in order to derail the wild dancing around the bonfires. (It didn't work.) My associations with Midsummer are also literary. My favorite play is Shakespeare's Midsummer Night's Dream, a romantical, farcical comedy in which fairies, Athenian nobles, and the lumpenproletariat all get involved in each others' love affairs. If it's been a long time since you've seen or read this play (which has also been filmed), find a copy and get reacquainted.

Midsummer is the longest day of the year, the day when the blazing, projective white light of the noon of the year burns strongest. If every day were Midsummer, the earth would be a global desert; even in this longest day, however, we know that the elements are elementally in balance and the shadows of the dark and the cold always lie behind the bright sunshine.

This is the day we tip back into night, and the traditional symbol of Midsummer is the ever-turning solar disk, which is an equal-armed cross inside a circle. You can make your own solar disk and hang it until Lammas above your altar or suspend it somewhere else in your house or in a tree in your yard. Buy a grapevine wreath at a craft store, soak it in warm water long enough to soften the vines, disassemble it, and reassemble it with the cross in the middle. Or make a wheel of wheat or straw. Use embroidery floss, yarn, or ribbons to bind two sticks and mount them inside a macrame or embroidery hoop likewise decorated. Wind long-stemmed silk flowers into a hoop and use more silk flowers to make the cross inside it. Cut your disk out of paper or a lacy gold paper doily or construction paper. Make a ribbon cross inside a ribbon-covered hoop made by bending a wire clothes hanger. However you make your solar disk, while you're working be mindful of what the disk represents and consider the circles and spirals of your life. Think about how you just keep rolling through your earthly life as the sun just keeps rolling across the sky. It gets up every morning and so do you.

Our Midsummer ritual (do it at noon if you can) focuses on personal power. Sometimes I'm not sure we have any. For millennia, we've been taught that the only real power resides in someone else who resides "up there." I say, let's bring some of that power back down here where we really live.

A very down-to-earth high priestess I know gives this assignment to people who come to study with her. The Gardnerian witches rede is "Do as thou wilt, an it harm none." What does it mean? She doesn't accept any mere paraphrase ("I can do anything I want to if I don't hurt anybody"), and she has told me that she often sends people back two or three times to consider the implications and ramifications of personal power and its use.

Make her assignment your assignment during the six weeks between Beltane and Midsummer. As you live and go about in the worlds of work and home and recreation, what powers do you have? What can you do? What effects do you have on other people? On the environment? Is anything you do like the famous butterfly effect of chaos theory wherein the flapping of a butterfly's wings in Peking can stir up a storm in New York? If you are powerful—strong, charismatic, smart, sexy, rich, etc.—so what?

Figure out what fiery power you have, what watery power, what airy power, what earthy power.

The powers of elemental fire are related to action and creativity. Are you a self-starter and an effective leader? Do you have a fiery temper that you release productively on behalf of "good" causes? Are you a poet, writer, musician, composer, artist, sculptor, dancer, or performance artist? Are you generally energetic? Do you generally walk the path of Experiential Play in your living?

The powers of elemental water are related to the emotions. Are you a loving person, an "earth mother" or "big daddy" to everyone who meets you, a volunteer in your community? Are you sensitive to others' moods and needs? Do your still waters run deeper than other people suspect, and are you more courageous than you yourself suspect? Do you generally follow the path of Devotion?

The powers of elemental air are related to the mind and learning. Are you intelligent, whether through formal education, reading and self-teaching, or street-smarts? Do you prefer rationality and logic to fuzzy emotionality? Do you understand such arcane sciences as quantum physics, chaos, and the farther reaches of computer science? Do you generally follow the path of Deep Thought?

The powers of elemental earth are related to groundedness and manifestation. Do you keep your feet firmly on the ground while all about you are spacing out? Are you a good cook or mechanic and can you fix things? Do you cherish tradition and work to heal the earth and its/her children? Do you understand that abundance means more than money? Do you generally follow the path of Good Works?

Write each description of your powers in red ink in one or two sentences on small pieces of white paper and lay them in the appropriate directions on your Midsummer altar.

Wear red for your Midsummer ritual and put red candles (as many as you want) on your altar. In the center, set a cauldron. It can be a little iron cauldron or a clay or ceramic bowl. Be sure your cauldron is reasonably heat-resistant and fill it half full with sand or cat litter.

Cast your circle, using the following invocations or your own words.

> Goddesses and gods of Fire
> Flaring, glowing elemental powers —
> Mighty ones who dance,
> Forceful ones who push
> the ever-turning wheel of creation,
> I welcome you.
> I am your sister/brother,
> and I bring my fiery powers
> to mingle with yours
> and celebrate the turning of the year.

Pick up the paper on which you described your fiery powers and read your words aloud. Then roll the paper into a funnel, light the open end at one of your red candles, and lay it on the sand in your cauldron. As it burns, visualize your power weaving into the solar disk and feel how your power flows with the all-encompassing power of the Goddess.

When the paper has been completely consumed, invoke the second elemental power.

> Goddesses and gods of Water
> Saturating, moistening elemental powers —

> Mighty ones who dance,
> Forceful ones who push
> the ever-turning wheel of creation,
> I welcome you.
> I am your sister/brother,
> and I bring my watery powers
> to mingle with yours
> and celebrate the turning of the year.

Pick up the paper on which you described your watery powers and read your words aloud. Then roll the paper into a funnel, light the open end, and lay it on the sand in your cauldron. As it burns, visualize your power weaving into the solar disk and feel how your power flows with the all-encompassing power of the Goddess.

When the paper has been completely consumed, invoke the third elemental power.

> Goddesses and gods of Air
> Gusting, breathing elemental powers—
> Mighty ones who dance,
> Forceful ones who push
> the ever-turning wheel of creation,
> I welcome you.
> I am your sister/brother,
> and I bring my airy powers
> to mingle with yours
> and celebrate the turning of the year.

Pick up the paper on which you described your airy powers and read your words aloud. Then roll the paper into a funnel, light the open end, and lay it on the sand in your cauldron. As it burns, visualize your power weaving into the solar disk and feel how your power flows with the all-encompassing power of the

Goddess.

When the paper has been completely consumed, invoke the fourth elemental power.

> Goddesses and gods of Earth
> Dark and solid elemental powers —
> Mighty ones who dance,
> Forceful ones who push
> the ever-turning wheel of creation,
> I welcome you.
> I am your sister/brother,
> and I bring my earthy powers
> to mingle with yours
> and celebrate the turning of the year.

Pick up the paper on which you described your earthy powers and read your words aloud. Then roll the paper into a funnel, light the open end, and lay it on the sand in your cauldron. As it burns, visualize your power weaving into the solar disk and feel how your power flows with the all-encompassing power of the Goddess.

When the paper has been completely consumed, invoke the Great Goddess (in your own words) or sing the Goddess Chant: ISIS, ASTARTE, DIANA, HECATE, DEMETER, KALI, INANNA.

If you know it, this is also a good time to sing the traditional African American spiritual "This little light of mine,/ I'm gonna let it shine." As you chant or sing, visualize your personal power mingling with the four elemental powers.

When you're ready, open your circle, ground yourself, and spend the rest of Midsummer's Eve and Day having a picnic and mingling with your friends. Go swimming, get a tan, make love, visit the zoo — have a good time.

10

RITUALS FOR THE GROWING DARK: WANING MOON, LAMMAS, FALL, HALLOWS

The power of the growing light has been projective, expressive, social, left-brained, outward-bound. When the sun and moon are waxing, it's time to plant metaphorical seeds and start new projects, it's time to put ourselves right out there and take action.

The power of the growing dark, on the other hand, will be receptive, more quietly expressive, solitary, right-brained, and inward-bound. When the sun and moon are waning, it's the time to come home, work on personal projects, harvest what has grown from our seeds, and bring closure to the big social projects. Nature goes underground during the dark and we come inside to rest.

The powers of light and dark are equal, and we must always be mindful of this fact. We must understand that the light = good / dark = bad dichotomy is false, racist, and sexist: the ideas of white and black powers, of white and black magic, are value-ridden and dangerous. It's the dancing of light and dark *together* that makes the wheel go round. If we were out in the light all the time, we'd never get any rest, but if we were inside, in the dark all the time, we'd get moldy. Too much bright white light creates deserts, too much deep darkness creates blindness.

For every birth there is a death, and for every death there is a rebirth. This is the lesson of light and dark.

Waning Moon Ritual: Release and Cleansing

We usually rest from ritual work during the two weeks from the full moon to the dark moon, when the light disappears altogether. We've been working hard since the new moon—planting seeds, raising power, luring love and attracting prosperity, drawing down the power of the full moon. Now it's time to pull back and take a break. If we work all the time, we'll burn out, and this can diminish our effectiveness when the moon turns again. We also need to give the powers of the cosmos time to move, for everything takes time to grow and manifest. We really must accept the concept of delayed gratification, however onerous it may be in an impatient world. So let's just relax and let things happen without our further help.

Take a break for two weeks. Read a good novel, go to the movies with friends you don't see often enough, return old phone calls and answer letters, attend to the things in your life that need your attention. If you want to, return to your projects in Goddess art, the ones you started in Chapter 2 and abandoned half-done.

If something comes up, however, we can still do rituals during a waning moon, as long as we keep in mind the fact that the magical tides are going out. If we do a ritual for love or money, for example, we should focus on letting go of unlovable feelings or deconstructing our mental blocks. Trying to do a forceful ritual is, to use the cliché, like trying to paddle upstream. We can do it, sure, but it's awfully hard work, and we may end up with strained muscles. So why not relax and "go with the flow"?

It's better to wait a couple of weeks, for the tides will turn.

They always do.

The following ritual is, accordingly, almost a nonritual. In your iron cauldron or clay bowl, which is half full of sand or cat litter, light a piece of self-igniting charcoal. While it's burning through, cast your circle so it's big enough to include your whole home.

When the charcoal is ready (like barbecue charcoal, it becomes gray and glowing), sprinkle a teaspoon of sage or sandalwood on it. If you don't have self-igniting charcoal, sage, or sandalwood, you can use a smudge stick. The best way I've found to ignite a smudge stick is to use the flame on the gas stove, but matches work, too. Gently blow on it to keep it going.

When you've got some good plumes and billows of incense, pick up your bowl (be careful) and a feather and walk in a *counterclockwise* direction all around your home, into every room, and fan incense or smudge into every corner. While you're doing this, chant SHE CHANGES EVERYTHING SHE TOUCHES. EVERYTHING SHE TOUCHES, CHANGES.

When you've made a complete circle around your home, stand or sit before your altar and purify yourself, too, stating aloud what you want to release from your life or consciousness. Breathe deeply a few times and open your circle. Set the smudge stick somewhere safe where it won't set anything on fire (red clay flowerpots are useful).

Lammas Celebration: Peace
July 31-August 1

With Lammas comes the beginning of the harvest season. The days are still long and it's probably hotter now than it was at Midsummer. These are the infamous "dog days," so called because the "dog star" Sirius rises and sets with the sun between mid-July and September.

The word "Lammas" comes from "loaf mass," which

celebrates the bread made from the first grain to be harvested. Another name for Lammas is Lughnasadh (pronounced approximately LOO-nus-uh), which means "commemoration of Lugh," the Celtic grain god. Like Baal, Lugh is a fire god, and his name may be related to Lucifer, the "light-bringer." In Irish legend, Lugh was a leader of the Tuatha De Danann, the people of the goddess Dana, as well as an artisan and patron of numerous towns, including Lyons and Leydon. Every year at harvest, Lugh is sacrificed so he can be reborn again. His sacrifice used to be celebrated with three days (or a month) of games and feasting and bonfires. Adonis and some of the other consorts/sons are also grain gods who are sacrificed, mourned, and reborn, and it is significant that Bethlehem means "house of bread."

There are also numerous grain goddesses. Ceres gives us our word "cereal," Freya is the Lady of the Loaf, and the Demeter/Persephone dyad is the Lady of the Threshing Floor, of the Seed, and of the Great Loaf. If this subject interests you, I recommend Pamela Berger's *The Goddess Obscured*, which traces the transmutation of the grain goddesses, including the Virgin Mary, into medieval saints.

As the foregoing might suggest, a traditional way to celebrate Lammas is with bread. Bake your own circular loaves into which you carve an equal-armed cross. If you don't want to start from scratch, buy "rise-and-bake" loaves or make cornbread muffins. I used to have a friend who made wonderful cornbread with blue cornmeal. She'd present it at a sabbat and go home with only crumbs left. You too can break bread with your friends on Lammas.

While the other three quarter days are still celebrated in popular culture, Lammas has somehow been neglected. We have Groundhog Day, May Day, and Halloween, but the only modern event to occur close to Lammas was the bombing of the Japanese cities Hiroshima and Nagasaki on August 6 and 9,

1945. These were the first times atomic bombs were dropped on civilian populations; the politicians and generals justified this horror by saying it ended World War II sooner. Maybe so.

If, like me, you've studied history, you probably suspect that ever since those first Indo-European warriors came galloping out of the Caucasian steppes and into the cities whose people worshipped the Great Goddess, it's been nothing but one war after another. That's more than 5,000 years of people killing each other over land that really belongs to the planet and over status symbols. Even relatively peaceful times like the Pax Romana and the Cold War were maintained by armies. History is written as a compilation of lists of kings and their conquests. The first "great book of the western world," *The Iliad*, is a song of war that praises the brutality of "heroes" like Achilles, Agamemnon, and Odysseus. Military heroes are people who kill other people.

All that's advanced today is the range of the weapons we use in our wars, and even though they look like video games now, our wars are still killing mothers and fathers and babies and grandparents and cousins.

I therefore propose a new Lammas ritual, one whose intention is to change the harvest of warfare to a gathering-in of peace.

Many people know and believe the stories about the medieval coven of England's New Forest. In 1588, they raised a cone of power that helped defeat the Spanish Armada. During World War II someone did it again, it's said, and helped save England from a Nazi invasion. I'm sure others have done similar things, too, though we seldom hear about them. If they can do it, why can't we do it?

Decorate your space and your altar in white, red, and black (the colors of the Triple Goddess), plus blue and green for peace and healing. Bring out your little globe from your spring ritual and put it back in the center. For music, the old African American spirituals are appropriate, also Suzanne Ciani or classical music like J.S. Bach's "Where Sheep May Safely Graze," or Phillip Glass's "Koyanisqaatsi." Dress in your robe, if you have one; if not, wear something comfortable that makes you feel powerful.

Light your candles and invoke the elemental powers.

> Holy Powers, Fiery Powers,
> Let there be peace on earth today.
>> Let men be gentle
>> Let women be courageous
>> Let children be playful.
> We are crying to you,
> I am calling to you:
>> Stay the firing of the weapons
>> Stop the building of the bombs.
> Bring peace to our sad and weary planet.

> Holy Powers, Watery Powers,
> Let there be peace on earth today.
>> Let men be gentle
>> Let women be courageous
>> Let children be playful.
> We are crying to you,
> I am calling to you:
>> Give the navies peaceful tasks
>> Drown the paths of battleships.
> Bring peace to our sad and weary planet.

> Holy Powers, Airy Powers,
> Let there be peace on earth today.
>> Let men be gentle

> Let women be courageous
> Let children be playful.
> We are crying to you,
> I am calling to you:
> Block the flights of missiles
> Ground every martial plane.
> Bring peace to our sad and weary planet.

> Holy Powers, Earthy Powers,
> Let there be peace on earth today.
> Let men be gentle
> Let women be courageous
> Let children be playful.
> We are crying to you,
> I am calling to you:
> Halt every marching army
> Fill every trench with grain.
> Bring peace to our sad and weary planet.

Next, invoke the Goddess, Queen of Heaven, Earth, and the Underworld. Ask Her to bless our planet and all Her children—two-legged, four-legged, many-legged, vegetable, and crystalline—with peace, joy, and harmony.

Build your cone of power out of the colors on your altar. Visualize it growing in height and power until it comes to climax, and then direct it to a troubled spot on earth. You have plenty of choices:

- the drug and gang wars in your own city and in most others
- the wars of occupation, as in Northern Ireland and Tibet
- the religious wars, as in Israel and India
- the genocidal wars, as in the former Yugoslavia
- the race wars, as in many U.S. cities
- the wars of suppression, as in China and the Mid-East

- the eco-wars, as in the redwood and rain forests and in the oceans
- the "civil" wars, as in Sri Lanka and the former Soviet Union
- the gender wars, as in the worlds of business, politics, and religion
- the propaganda wars around the world

When you're ready, open your circle and ground your energy. You can do this by singing the beautiful New Thought song, "Let There Be Peace on Earth." When you come to the "God our Father" line, however, rephrase it as follows:

With the Goddess, our Mother,
Children all are we.
Let us dance with each other
In peace and harmony.

Fall Celebration: Harvest
September 20-23

At both equinoxes, time is in balance. These are the two days of the year that are just as long as their nights. What we planted last spring, we reap this fall: nature gives us a lesson in the meaning of karma.

Another name for the autumnal equinox, Mabon, comes from Queen Mab of the Fairies, also the Celtic Queen Maeve, heroine of one of the Irish epics (In *Romeo and Juliet*, Mercutio describes Queen Mab as being "no bigger than an agate-stone" in an alderman's ring. Thus are the goddesses diminished.)

Other celebrations occur around the equinox: the Swiss Pilgrimage of the Black Virgins; the birthdays of the Eskimo Crone, Sedna, and of St. Hildegard of Bingen (1098–1179); and Michaelmas, a British holiday that commemorates St.

Michael/Lucifer, the Light-Bringer. We can read Hildegard's visions and listen to her music as we see the Light-Bringer's glory in the blaze of dying leaves. Rosh Hashanah and Yom Kippur also fall in late September or early October (1 or 2 Tishri and 10 Tishri in the Hebrew calendar). Rosh Hashanah is New Year, and Yom Kippur is the Day of Atonement, when, originally, the tribes sacrificed goats to the god Azazel; this custom is also related to the death of Tammuz.

The fall equinox marks the first day of Libra (whose scales are Ma'at's or Astraea's) and the Greater Eleusinian Mysteries, which was the most famous religious festival of the ancient world. Lasting nine days, it was open to anyone who hadn't committed murder, and it was celebrated at the Greek city of Eleusis, a day's walk from Athens. (For the PBS series *Voyages* in 1990, English historian Michael Wood walked along the route the initiates took from Athens to Eleusis; try to catch this excellent program in rerun.) It was in Eleusis that Demeter, mourning the loss of Persephone, took a job as nursemaid for Triptolemos, infant son of Queen Metanira. Demeter tried to make the boy immortal by smoking him in the fireplace; his mother objected, and the goddess relented but continued to mourn until the queen's daughter Baubo exposed her vulva and made her laugh. Demeter now revealed herself as a goddess and taught Triptolemos the arts of agriculture; he built a temple in her honor and established the Mysteries. Even though thousands of people were initiated, *no one ever broke the vow of secrecy*, so all we know today is what scholars have gleaned from literature and other sources. One of the best present-day descriptions appears in Durdin-Robertson's *Year of the Goddess*.

Mabon is the Witches Thanksgiving. The last grain harvested is plaited into a corn dolly, called the Corn Mother. She's kept in a place of honor through the winter and becomes the Corn Bride at Candlemas, when she's mated with the reborn

Corn King. In Egypt, the Nile crests at its greatest height in late September, promising future fertility.

In the light there is always a seed of dark, and in the dark there is always a seed of light. Planting and harvesting are two stations on the ever-turning wheel of the year. Our fall ritual is a harvest celebration.

Decorate your home and your altar with dried wheat, gourds, colored corn, and fall leaves and flowers. Use candles in fall colors: greens, gold, yellow, orange, scarlet, dark red. If you have a corn dolly, lay it in the center of your altar as your goddess symbol. Since the climax of the Eleusinian Mysteries was the revelation of a grain of corn (actually wheat or barley in Europe; what we call "corn" is Native American maize) and a whispered message about the link between death and birth, you can also use a single head of wheat for your goddess symbol. Lay it on a plain clay saucer.

Because you're celebrating your own harvest, gather the fruits of all the things you've "planted" since the last fall equinox. These can be photos of new children or grandchildren, certificates or diplomas you've earned, your marriage or divorce documentation, proposals that actually landed contracts and contracts you've signed, purchases you've made, and any kind of project at or near completion. Pile all this stuff on your altar (out of range of the burning candles) so you can see *how much* you've planted and harvested. One arrangement would be to heap everything in the center and put the goddess symbol on the top of the heap. The idea is not neatness; it's fruitfulness.

Invoke the four elemental powers and the Goddess, thanking them for all blessings and gifts they've brought into your life during the past year and asking them to continue blessing you.

Next, lay your hands on your piled-up harvest and read the following blessing or use it as a model to make up your own words.

This is my harvest,
    and I give thanks.
These things are the fruits of a year of my life,
    and I give thanks.
With the blessings of the Goddess
And through my own hard work,
    I have planted my seeds
    I have watered and weeded tender growth
    I have guided the strong young shoots
    I have thinned out the weak ones that would not live
    I have enjoyed my flowerings
    I have loved the fruits of my work.
And now at harvest time,
    I give thanks.
These are my most perfect fruits:
    I lay them on Her altar in gratitude
    I lay them on Her altar in hope
    I lay them on Her altar in blessing.
For what we harvest now, we plant again next spring.

Finally, sing the old, familiar Thanksgiving song, which you probably learned (as I did) in the second or third grade. I've rewritten it slightly.

Come, ye thankful people, come,
Raise the song of Harvest Home;
All is safely gathered in
Ere the winter storms begin;
Holy Goddess doth provide
For our wants to be supplied;
Come to Her own temple come,
Raise the song of Harvest Home.
First the blade and then the ear,

Then the full grain doth appear.
Grant, o Harvest Lord, that we
Wholesome grain and pure may be.
Come, ye thankful people, come,
Raise the song of Harvest Home.
Come to Her own temple, come,
Raise the song of Harvest Home.

You can also do this ritual for the Harvest Moon, which is the full moon that falls nearest the fall equinox.

Hallows Celebration: Honoring Our Dead
October 31-November 1

How many of the kids who put on their Teenage Mutant Ninja Turtles and Freddy Krueger costumes and thrust plastic bags at us for candy know what "trick or treat" really means? Do they know that Halloween is our most sacred holiday? Do they know why they dress as ghosts and witches and carry plastic jack-o'-lanterns?

Today, alas, it's only party time.

But it hasn't always been so.

Hallows, Hallowmas, All Hallows Eve—the "hallow" in all three names comes from the Middle English word that means "holy." When something is hallowed, it is sanctified and consecrated. Even when the Christian Church took over our holiday (holy day), it kept the name, for "Halloween" means "hallowed evening." Not only that, they also made November 1 All Saints Day and November 2 All Souls Day.

The traditional Celtic name is Samhain (pronounced approximately SOW-en, "sow" rhyming with "cow"). Samhain may mean "summer's end," or it may be named after Samana, an Aryan death god who is the Grim Reaper and leader of the ghosts of our ancestors. Samana's name is also echoed in the

Bible as Samuel, whose name is related to the Semitic god of the Underworld, Samael. A Samael also appears in the Gnostic Gospels as a fool.

Other festivals occur at the end of October, when anything not harvested is left in the fields for the Pooks and other Old Ones to gather, and livestock not likely to survive the winter is slaughtered to provide food for the community. One festival is the Latin American *El Dia de las Muertes* (Day of the Dead), actually a week-long festival. You may be familiar with the sugar skulls, the graveyard feasts, and wonderful *ofrenda* altars. An enduring ancient festival was the Isia, a week-long observance of Isis's search for and recovery of her brother/husband Osiris. Isis was arguably the most widely worshipped goddess of the Greco-Roman world, and many events in her story were appropriated into the Christian myth. Inanna, too, is in the Underworld at this time. She's been hanging for three days on the meat hook in her sister Ereshkigal's palace, and Ninshubur, her handmaiden or prime minister,[32] is now beginning her or his search and rescue mission. Inanna's lover, Dumuzi, will be given to Ereshkigal in her place, since the numbers of living and dead cannot be out of balance.

Although the door (or veil or crack) between the worlds of the living and the dead is ajar on all four quarter days, it's open widest at Hallows. This is the night when the dead return to visit, feast, and tell us what they see from their perspective.

Hallows is the festival of the Crone, the aged mother and grandmother, the wise old one, our healer, our counselor, our judge. Today we see Her on cards and decorations as a warty, wicked old witch flying on her broomstick with her familiars, the owl and the black cat, across the full moon, with ghosts and jack-o'-lanterns lurking in the dry fields below. All these details are holdovers from pagan beliefs.

Also associated with Hallows are Persephone's pomegranate, the apple whose seeds form a natural pentacle, and pumpkins carved into scary faces both to provide light to Witches going to their sabbat and to discourage the over-curious nonbeliever.

A major symbol of Hallows is the cauldron. On a practical level, it's a cooking pot, though, yes, perhaps it has also been used for potions such as *Macbeth's* Weird Sisters are portrayed as stirring up. Originally, however, the cauldron is the Crone's container, the pot in which churning, boiling chaos is stirred up to disintegrate and reintegrate dead matter—plants, animals, us, everything. The cauldron represents the womb of the Goddess, from which we will all be reborn.

Whether it's a commercialized holiday or a true holy day, Hallows is a celebration of the link between the living and the dead. Stop for a minute and consider all the stories of dying and reborn vegetation gods and goddesses. Ponder the fact that directly opposite Hallows/Halloween on the wheel of the year is Beltane, that wonderful, exuberant celebration of light and life.

Because Hallows is so popular (where I live, kids start knocking on doors at four in the afternoon), you probably need two celebrations. Hold your party early, invite your friends and their kids to come in costume, play games, and engage in tricks and treats. Originally, the treat was the food left for the ancestors and the fairies; forget their treat, and they'd play tricks on you, probably all year. After the party animals have all gone home and no one's stalking your doorbell anymore, hold your Hallows ritual. The Campanellis' *Wheel of the Year* gives a beautiful account of Hallows lore and parties.

Our quiet ritual, then, is to honor our dead.

The first part of the ritual is the construction of an ancestor altar. Decide where you want to put it, either in temporary residence on your working altar, on a table, or in a more private place. Mine is the top of a bookcase in my bedroom. Before you begin the altar, invite the elemental powers into your space, asking for their blessings on you and your ancestors.

Next, find photos of your honored dead. These can be ancestors, family members or friends who have died in wars or from AIDS or other catastrophes, or other people you care about—anyone who is now living in Persephone's realm. If ancestors, try to find photos taken when they were young. On my altar are a thirty-year-old collar from my first cat, a photo of my mother, and a photo of my grandparents holding me when I was two months old; in this photo, my grandmother (who died at age 95 in January, 1991) was five years younger than I am now. Make a collage of these photos in one large frame or arrange them in small individual frames. Your goal is to use the most beautiful frames you can find (borrow them if necessary) to honor these people. Add your chalice or another small glass of water to the altar, and an indigo or deep purple candle in a beautiful holder. If you want to, add other beautiful things and special symbols: a family memento, a ceramic snake or egg to symbolize rebirth, a dried pomegranate or some wheat, dried or fresh flowers, anything else your honored dead will enjoy. My altar has an antique glass nest egg, a sprig of pussy willow in memory of the tree in my grandparents' backyard and a clay bead with a spiral design.

Work in a worshipful frame of mind with quiet music and soft lighting. Make this the most beautiful altar you can create. Even if you will take it down tomorrow or (preferably) on November 2, know that your honored dead deserve such beauty, and remember that taking the altar down reflects the fact that life ends in death ... and next year, when you create a new ancestor altar, rebirth.

If you can find one, get a fresh pomegranate and have it ready, cut in half, on a beautiful dish. You will eat the seeds of one half and leave the other for your ancestors. If you can't find a pomegranate, cut an apple in half horizontally and have it ready on the dish.

When you're pleased with your ancestor altar, light the candle and sit quietly, establishing a helix of indigo or deep purple energy around your sacred space. Feel it moving in a gentle, stately flow.

Eat two or three pomegranate seeds or take a bite of the apple and invoke the Crone.

> Honored Crone, Gracious Hecate,
> Grandmother Guardian of the Maiden and the Son,
> Sarah, Sedna, Sibyl, Old One, teller of the wise tales,
> Baba Yaga, dweller in the last sheaf of grain,
> De Anna, Grandmother of God —
> I call on you in your many forms:
> Bring comfort to the ones I love
> until they are born again.
> Honored Crone, I ask Your blessing and compassion
> for their souls
> and for my own.

Now invoke the dead people. This is *not* a seance, nor are you channeling bodiless space entities. You will not see ghosts or hear mysterious voices or rapping tables. This is a simple ritual in which you can tell your honored dead the things that you wanted to tell them when they still lived here on earth, but never quite got around to saying.

Eat a few more pomegranate seeds (or more of the apple).

> Honored Ones who have gone before me —
> [name them all, use the pet names you used to share] —
> Tonight is the night we celebrate together,
> Tonight we can be together once more

in peace and love and friendship
for our measure of time.
I welcome you.
Be comfortable in my circle.

Pause, eat a few more seeds or more apple, and imagine these people joining you, sitting comfortably with you in your circle. Feel the love and comfort you all share again.

Eat a few more of the pomegranate seeds and remember that when Persephone eats such seeds, she is kept in the Realm of the Dead for her measure of time. Eat two or three more seeds and remember that she is reborn every year at Candlemas.

In the pre-Olympian version of her story, Persephone is not kidnapped. She hears cries and moans, the wistful voices of the unhappy dead, coming up through a crevice in the earth, and she voluntarily goes down to visit them. Does no one care for these shadowy spirits? Does no one remember them? She gives them as much comfort as she can, but there are so many and she is so compassionate that she refuses to rejoin her own grieving mother until she has done as much as she can in the Underworld, but she promises to return to earth every fall.

Eat a few more seeds or more apple and retell this story, in your own words, to your guests.

Talk to them, one by one, and tell them all the current news, the gossip about the people they used to know, the things they used to care about. Tell them how it is with you. Tell them what you wanted to tell them before they died, but for whatever reason could not say at that time. Pause, eat a few more pomegranate seeds, and listen with your inner ears to what they have to say to you. Take as much time with this part of the ritual as you need, and if you cry, wipe your eyes and remember that crying is an important expression of feelings.

Finally, say good-bye to each person. You may not have

done that before, either. Release each person from hurts and angers and denials. Tell these people from your life that you realize that they live in Persephone's realm now, and that you understand. You *do* understand. Let go of everything but the love. Give them permission to go on to new lives, even though you may not see them again.

Open your circle. Leave the other half of the pomegranate or apple on your altar next to the water for your honored dead to feast upon. Extinguish the candle and ground yourself.

During the afternoon of November 2, destroy your ancestor altar. That is, take it apart with as much love and joy as you created it, knowing that you can re-create it next year. Bury the ancestors' half of the pomegranate or apple under your tree and water it with their water.

11

RITUALS FOR
THE DEEP DARK:
DARK MOON, YULETIDE

It was morning when we began our tour of the calendar. It was the new moon, Candlemas, the year's morning. We moved with the powers of the growing light, got brighter with the sun, sounded forth at noon, did all the things we had to do while it was still light. We see more clearly in the noon light, so we did the outward things the world can see.

Now we're facing the dark. The light's been turned off and it's time to go to bed. But remember—it's dark inside a seed, it's dark inside an egg, it's dark inside the cave where the bear's hibernating and under the mud where the frog's asleep. It's dark inside our mother's womb and in our cozy warm bed with the covers pulled up. It's dark in the theatre while the play's the thing and the film's running.

It's the dark moon, Yuletide, the year's midnight. It's the Witching Hour.

And if you listen very carefully and count the months of the moon, you'll hear the clock strike thirteen.

Dark Moon Ritual: Reversing

When the last sliver of the waning moon disappears, it's the dark moon, and in practical terms we have two or three days for dark moon work before the dark moon slides into new. Every month, the Crone bathes in the fountain of rebirth and is reborn as the Maiden, who grows up, becomes the Mother, and then grows old again.

Even though we can't see it, the dark moon's power is just as strong as the full moon's. It's the same power, only now it's different, and the difference lies in the direction of the flow. The full moon is high tide and manifestation, the dark moon is low tide and release. (Yes, in the ocean, the low tides are at the quarter moons; we're speaking of psychic tides here.) The work we do under the dark moon, therefore, is reversing and banishing work, and the goddesses we invoke are the crones and goddesses of justice and retribution: Ma'at, Themis, Astraea, Oya, Deborah, Nemesis, the Erinyes, the Fates, the Norns.

This is not the time to work out of personal pique or petty anger. Using a reversing ritual on the jerk who wouldn't let you on the freeway or the neighbor who plays grunge rock at midnight is like the clichéd phrase, using an elephant gun on a mouse. For things like this, don't use magic. Call the cops.

Above all, when you do reversing rituals, remember that what you put out comes back, at least threefold, maybe more. Be very clear that the energy that's being reversed is *the offender's own energy*. You're a mirror, and it's quite likely, in fact, that you'll never know exactly what happens as a result of your reversing ritual. You don't need to know. Punishment is between the offender and the Crone, and the details are up to Her.

The dark moon is the time to work for *justice*, which can be both personal and social. For example, if a client or business refuses to pay you for services rendered, if a manufacturer or distributor of shoddy merchandise won't repair or replace it, if you've truly been attacked or abused, try appropriate correspondence to the right authorities, try personal appeals, try legal remedies. And, in addition, zap 'em with a reversing ritual.

Or if a developer and his accountants are dividing up the local wetlands, if someone is "spilling" oil on the beach, if someone is trying to coerce a woman into giving up her reproductive freedom, if someone is trying to revive the Inquisition (and we who are out of the broomcloset know that the Inquisition never really died), write letters, join demonstrations, participate in economic boycotts, send money to Greenpeace, NARAL, or PETA. And, in addition, zap 'em with a reversing ritual.

Buy a reversing candle at your local magical supply store. A reversing candle has a red core surrounded by black, though beeswax reversing candles are red and black wound together. If you can't find a reversing candle, use a plain black candle. If the candle is more than four to six inches tall, cut it to that size, since for a reversing ritual the candle must burn all the way down and you won't want to be sitting there with it all day or all night. Save the other half for another ritual. If you use a plain candle, scratch the offender's name in it, using a knife or a thorn or a rusty nail; if you're using beeswax, write the offender's name on a small piece of paper and lay it in the saucer under the candle.

If you have the offender's signature, photocopy it and cut around it so it's a small piece of paper. Wrap it in black thread. It will be burned during the ritual. If you have the offender's business card, wrap it in black thread, also to be burned.

Anchor your reversing candle on a brass or clay saucer, then sprinkle a pinch of one or more of the following herbs over the candle. These are all traditionally used for exorcism, purification, or protection. You are exorcising the offender's energy from your life, purifying both his and your own energies, and protecting yourself. Use basil, bay leaf, anise, sage, rosemary, and mixed salt and pepper. Ideally, we might use herbs ruled by Saturn to take advantage of that god's binding power, but most of Saturn's herbs are both extremely poisonous and generally unavailable. *Never use dangerous herbs* in a ritual. It's just not worth the risk to your health.

After you've sprinkled the herbs over the candle, pour about a teaspoon of olive oil over it. Be sure to protect your altar from the mess all this may make.

Have your cauldron, half full of sand or cat litter, ready on your altar.

Light the reversing candle and visualize the red and black energies rising like snakes, swirling around above the candle, and then traveling out to find the offender. Invoke the elemental powers.

> Powers of Fire
> Be present for my work tonight.
> [Name of offender] has offended Justice.
> [Name] has [describe the offense, giving names, dates,
>   amounts, and other details].
> Mighty Powers of Fire,
> As you move through our world,
> Use your invisible cleansing flames
> To burn away [name's] offense.
> Let the harm [name] has done be returned to [name]
>   in full measure
>   no more, no less
>   without rancor, without pity.
> As I demand justice,
> So must it be.

Powers of Water
Be present for my work tonight.
[Name of offender] has offended Justice.
[Name] has [describe the offense, giving names, dates,
    amounts, and other details].
Mighty Powers of Water,
As you move through our world,
Use your invisible tides
To wash away [name's] offense.
Let the harm [name] has done be returned to [name]
        in full measure
        no more, no less
        without rancor, without pity.
As I demand justice,
So must it be.

Powers of Air
Be present for my work tonight.
[Name of offender] has offended Justice.
[Name] has [describe the offense, giving names, dates,
    amounts, and other details].
Mighty Powers of Air,
As you move through our world,
Use your invisible winds
To blow away [name's] offense.
Let the harm [name] has done be returned to [name]
        in full measure
        no more, no less
        without rancor, without pity.
As I demand justice,
So must it be.

Powers of Earth
Be present for my work tonight.
[Name of offender] has offended Justice.
[Name] has [describe the offense, giving names, dates,
    amounts, and other details].
Mighty Powers of Earth,
As you move through our world,
Use your invisible force
To bury [name's] offense.
Let the harm [name] has done be returned to [name]
        in full measure
        no more, no less
        without rancor, without pity.
As I demand justice,
So must it be.

Next, invoke one or more of the goddesses of Justice named earlier. Here's an example:

Implacable Hecate, Invincible Ma'at,
Grandmothers of Justice,
I cry out to You.
[Name] has offended You.
Let [name] reap what he has sown,
Let [name] pay his debts to Justice,
Let [name] change his ways.

Light the piece of paper with his signature on it or his business card (or both) in the flame of the reversing candle and let them burn to ashes in your cauldron.

Wise Ones, Old Ones, Relentless Ones —
Bring [name] to Justice.

Let the harm [name] has done be returned to [name]
    in full measure
    no more, no less
    without rancor, without pity.
As [name] has sown harm,
As I demand Justice,
So mote it be.

This next part is very important. Visualize a silver sphere rising from the reversing candle, a sphere whose inner surface is an unbroken mirror. In your imagination, send this sphere to the offender's office or home (or both) and watch it grow large enough to completely surround the office or home. You have created a spherical mirror around the offender, and every harmful thought, word, or action the offender sends out will ricochet around and through him or her again and again. If you want to, you can check in and renew this sphere each dawn and dusk for as long as you think necessary.

Use a rattle or drum to stir up the energy or sit quietly as the candle burns down. Be sure to think about justice, not revenge. This ritual isn't over until the candle has burned down completely, though you can extinguish the flame when there's only a puddle of wax. Put this in your freezer. Keep it there.

Open your circle and be sure to ground yourself. If you want to, burn some rosemary or sage (for cleansing) in your cauldron.

Yuletide Celebration: Rest and Revival
December 18–January 6

Even though the stores have had their Christmas decorations and sales up and going since the middle of October and we may be booked for twice as many Christmas and New Year parties as we can really cope with, the true center of this season is the winter solstice (as usual, check your calendar for the exact date). It's the longest night of the year, and since this season is ruled by Saturn, it's the time when, deep down, we really want to stay home and take a nice long nap.

With catholic abandon, I extend the holiday so I can celebrate with everybody and still keep enough time for myself. Some of the social holidays are the ancient Roman festival of Saturnalia (a week of carnival beginning December 18), Kwanzaa (a week-long African American celebration), Hanukkah (eight days), Yule (the Gothic 12-day winter celebration), and both Christmas itself (December 25) and the Twelve Days of Christmas (ending on January 6). I put it all together and call the collective holiday Yuletide.

Saturnalia, which antedated the Roman Empire, was named after Saturn, who is both Father Time, the Grim Reaper, and the god of agriculture and ruler of the Golden Age. His wife is Ops, whose name and attributes survive in our word *opulent;* her special holiday was December 19. During the Saturnalia, society was turned upside-down: laws were suspended and the courts were closed, school was out, wars were even put on hold. Nobody worked during the reign of the Lord of Misrule. It was carnival, party time, time for pranks and practical jokes, time to whoop it up.

Kwanzaa is a modern African American alternative to Christmas. During this cultural (not religious) holiday, people light a candle each day and celebrate aspects of traditional African life. The seven candles represent the seven principles of life, in Swahili called the *Nguzo Saba:* unity, self-determination, responsibility, cooperative economics, purpose, creativity, and faith. Another feast with multiple lights is Hanukkah, which falls on 25 Kislev in the Hebrew calendar; it's the Festival of Lights that commemorates the Maccabean rededication of the temple in Jerusalem, at which time a one-day supply of lamp oil lasted eight days. Both of these holidays fall at the winter solstice and both are dedicated to light, enlightenment, and remembrance.

Christmas (in Middle English *Cristes Maess*) is another example of how the Christian bishops adopted pagan holidays and symbols. Since the people were accustomed to celebrating in December, the fathers of the church took advantage of the custom but changed its object. Christmas was first celebrated (on January 6) some 350 years after the birth it commemorates; a century later, the date of the birth of Jesus (who was actually born in Nazareth) was moved to December 25, which is also the birthday of Mithra. The solstice is, in fact, the birthday of a dozen or more solar gods: Aeon, Attis, Baldur, Chango, Dionysus, Frey, Helios, Horus, Jesus, Mithra, Osiris, Quetzalcoatl, Tammuz. Their mother is the Celestial Queen, and the Romans called the occasion the Birthday of the Unconquerable Sun. The night before, by the way, is dedicated to the Mothers. Madranicht (Mothers Night) is the Celtic and Germanic celebration of home, hearth, and fertility.

Yule comes from the Old English *geol* and from similar Norse and Saxon words that mean "wheel," as in the zodiac or wheel of life and the year whose eight spokes are our eight festivals. The turning of the wheel is the informing concept in this winter holiday: time itself, as everyone (except the linear rationalist) knows, is a wheel that includes our reincarnational lives as well as all the cycles of nature on earth and in the skies.

Light is equally important. As we have seen, light and dark dance together during the year, approaching and retreating and revolving together in their times. Before we got central heating and electric lights, the winter solstice (which is also the first day of Capricorn) was possibly the most fearsome night of the year. Imagine sitting by the hearthfire or the rushlights listening to the wind and watching your food stores getting smaller and smaller. Would the light really return? Would the warmth really come back? Would the family, clan, or tribe survive the hard times? Would they live until the next growing season and its harvest? These doubts may be responsible for the solstice celebrations: "Eat, drink, and carry on, for we may not make it through the winter."

Believing that the Sun Goddess, the Mother of Plants and Animals, always provided and that the son/sun would always be reborn was genuine cause for celebration. It must also have been a genuine trial of faith. Long before St. John of the Cross, winter must have been a dark night of the soul as well as the sky.

Our Yuletide ritual requires no soul's dark night, but it may give you a sweet nap.

Decorate your home and your altar with any or all of the familiar seasonal symbols. Start with candles, a multitude in red, green, white, and especially silver and gold. Scented candles are wonderful, or you can burn a Yule incense or pine, bayberry, or holiday spice potpourri. Pick a scent you really love. Even if you're not Jewish or African American, find a place in your home for a many-branched candelabra and light a candle a day to join our sisters and brothers in celebrating their lights. The evergreens that smell so good remind us that life never dies, and the Christmas tree reminds us that all trees are sacred to the Goddess. The lights in the tree represent the sun, moon, and stars, the lights of the dead, and perhaps the Goddess Herself dancing in the Northern Lights. The holly is named after Frau Holle (or Hel), a northern underground goddess who is the grandmother/comforter of all babies; the ivy is a symbol of Dionysus and eternal life; and mistletoe was holy to the Druids.

Santa Claus is a shaman. He wears the three sacred colors of the Triple Goddess and he's fat because he's well-fed. (A traditional shaman once told me that you should never trust a skinny shaman; if his people don't provide for him, he's not doing his job.) Santa flies from the frozen north, where the Saami, or Lapp, shamans still wield their full, traditional power, and he is drawn through the air behind his sacred, magical reindeer whose antlers symbolize the surging force of life. His gifts are the gifts of the spirit made material. In this context, the Christmas tree is the world pole, for from Mongolia to the American Southwest, shamans customarily ascend tent poles or trees when they make their astral journeys. Santa knows everything, especially if we've been good or bad, and like karma itself, he gives us our just desserts. His attendants, the toy-making elves, are the Old Ones. Be sure, therefore, to give Santa a place on your altar, too.

Although the purpose of any ritual is to alter our consciousness, some rituals involve more than sitting before an altar and invoking energies. Sometimes ritual is drama. Drama historians believe that drama was born in ritual, that is, in sympathetic magic that acted out hunts and other important occasions. Greek drama was born in celebrations to Dionysus and on the threshing floor, which became the circular arena on which the Greek chorus danced, and modern drama was born on the porches of the medieval cathedrals as mystery and miracle plays. Our Yuletide ritual is thus a little play, and you get to be all the characters.

Because this ritual is about rest and revival, you need a blanket, preferably an old, handmade quilt or comforter full of warm and snuggly associations. You can also use a baby blanket or anything else that will cover at least part of your body.

You also need a small gift to yourself. This can be a crystal, a flower, a book, any small item you really want. It's your gift from the Goddess Ops, so wrap it as beautifully as you'd wrap a gift to anyone else you love. Lay it on the altar. For music, Benjamin Britten's "A Ceremony of Carols" is beautiful. It's available in several taped versions.

Light your silver candle and sit on your blanket. Cast your circle by inviting the elemental powers to celebrate the long winter's night with you. Ask them to take the same places the guardian angels take around Hansel and Gretel in Humperdinck's opera, watching over you at your head, feet, right and left hands, above you and below you.

Draw your blanket up over your shoulders, as if to shelter yourself from bad weather and the cold, and invoke Frau Holle into your circle. I always picture her kind of like Cinderella's Fairy Godmother from the Disney movie. Address her as Grandmother and ask her to comfort you and cradle you on her generous lap.

> Frau Holle, Grandmother of All,
> it's winter, and I am cold.
> Frau Holle, Grandmother of All,
> it's dark, and I am weary.
> Frau Holle, Grandmother of All,
> take me in your arms —
> hold me, rock me, cradle me,
> and watch me while I sleep.

If your blanket is big enough, lie down and roll up in it. At least curl up in front of your altar and pull the blanket around your shoulders. As you tuck yourself in, imagine Frau Holle coming to tuck you in and sing you a lullaby—the aria from *Hansel & Gretel*, "All Through the Night," Brahms' Lullaby, "Mockingbird," or any other lullaby you know. As Frau Holle, sing it to yourself.

When she has finished singing to you, Frau Holle sits in her old rocking chair and takes out her eternal knitting, which becomes the blanket of snow that covers the land.

Now, warm and snuggly in your own blanket, you get to be

an animal. You're a bear in your cave, some smaller animal in your burrow. You've eaten enough to sustain you through the winter, you've grown a heavy coat of glossy fur to keep you warm, and you know it's time for your rest. Peek out of your burrow at the shining moon (the silver candle on your altar), then curl up again and go to sleep. You may actually fall asleep. If you do, make sure ahead of time that your candle is safe, on a holder that absolutely won't burn and away from anything flammable on your altar.

When you wake up, make animal noises. Yawn and stretch. Winter's over! The sun has been reborn! Untangle yourself from your blanket and crawl out of your cave under the earth. Light your gold candle and greet the newborn sun.

> Hail, golden Saule, beautiful Hathor,
> mighty Mithra, gentle Jesus.
> Hail, climbing power of the rising sun,
> living day, illumination, warming joy.
> Night is done, winter's over,
> I rejoice! Welcome, rising sun!

Frau Holle returns, but with the passing of winter she's been transformed! She's become your Christmas tree angel, and now she's on the top of the tree, singing and dancing. The angel has a gift for you. As the angel, descend from the Goddess's tree of life and rebirth and give yourself the gift that you just happen to find on the altar. As yourself again, exclaim over the beauty of the packaging, unwrap the gift, and thank the Goddess Ops for giving you exactly what you wanted. If you see Santa Shaman hovering nearby, thank him, too.

Spend a few minutes sitting on your blanket, holding your gift, and thinking about your long winter's nap and your joyous revival. Think about what this sleep and rebirth have meant to you, and give thanks once more that the wheel of the year has turned again, as it eternally and inevitably does. Sing another song. (This is the familiar Christmas carol, slightly rewritten.)

> Joy to the world,
> The light is born.
> Let earth begin to sing.
> Let every heart
> Rejoice in the light.
> And heaven and nature sing,
> And heaven and nature sing,
> And heaven, and earth, and nature sing!

For the rest of Yuletide, share your joy with your family and friends.

AFTERWORD

In his "spiritual maxims," Brother Lawrence defines the practice of the presence of God as he sees and lives it:

We must continually work hard so that each of our actions is a way of carrying on little conversations with God, not in any carefully prepared way but as it comes from the purity and simplicity of the heart.

You and I who love the Goddess look at a tree every day, at the moon every night. By day, we see bare branches against the sky, and soon we see the tiny, shiny green leaves. The weather gets warmer and we see full growth and blossoms and fruit, and finally we see dry leaves falling to the ground. By night, we see the changes of the moon, we see the "man in the moon," and we discover where the moon moves across the sky during the year.

The Goddess and us—we're carrying on a wordless conversation all the time, a conversation in our hearts and in all our senses. The Queen of Heaven, Earth, and the Underworld is beautiful. The Lady of the Plants and Animals is present to us, too. The mama of hearth and earth loves us as we love her.

We've come through a year in the Goddess together now, and we've explored thealogy, mystery, and play. We've touched the layers and manifestations of the Great Goddess and celebrated and worshipped and played with Her. Wherever anything is, there She is.

And you — you've been initiated, by and for yourself; no one else had to do it for you. You've erected and built your altars and your powers, you've worked for the earth and for peace and justice. You know how to plant your seeds of hope and harvest your crops, you know how to talk to dead people, and you know how to work and rest, and when.

You know what a ritual is, and you know that you can create your own rituals.

You've completed my book and you're on your own now, except you're not alone. But you know that, too.

Let me end by paraphrasing three wise old sisters who perhaps danced together once upon a time upon a heath:

> Bright blessings,
> Gentle blessings,
> Magical blessings —
> Thrice to thine, and thrice to mine
> And thrice again to make up nine.
> Peace! the charm's wound up.

Barbara Ardinger, Ph.D.
Hallows, 1994

NOTES

1. Books mentioned in the text are listed in the Bibliography.

2. "Thealogy," like "ovular" and "hera," are words used in the writings of women's spirituality to bring a feminine dimension into our largely masculine language, just as the revival of the ancient goddesses brings a feminine dimension to the largely patriarchal religions.

3. "Hera" has been suggested by several feminist authors as the proper alternative to "female hero." Joan of Arc is a hera. So are Emma Goldman and Georgia O'Keeffe. So are my mother and your mother.

4. As I originally wrote this line, it said, "I bless the nine million." *That nine million women burned is a myth.* I too believed it until I learned better. We know that from the records that the population of all of Europe before the Black Death (1349) may have reached 20 million souls, but the plague and the Hundred Years War killed one-third to one-half of them, and during the "little ice age" the population did not grow quickly. There just weren't nine million women left to burn. A more accurate number of deaths may be 50,000 to 100,000. It cannot be denied, however, that in areas like Germany, Austria, France, northern Italy, and southern England, where the Catholics and Protestants were most actively killing each other, the persecution was terrible and villages were left with just one or two living women in them. The nine million was "concocted" says John Yohalem, editor of *Enchanté*, in 1951 by Cecil Williamson, founder of the Witchcraft Museum on the Isle of Man. "He seems to have reached this number by turning the number of Jews slain by the Nazis upside down."

5. See Margot Adler's *Drawing Down the Moon* for examples of all sorts of Neo-Pagans.

6. See the list of resources at the end of this book and *The Womanspirit Sourcebook.*

7. See the list of resources at the end of this book and *The Womanspirit Sourcebook.*

8. John Tierney, et al., "The Search for Adam and Eve," *Newsweek* (Jan. 11, 1988) pp. 46-52.

9. See the list of resources for information.

10. See the list of resources for periodicals that advertise workshops.

11. See Discography.

12. See Discography.

13. Toni Head, "Changing Hymns to Hers," in *The Great Goddess, Heresies* (Vol. 2, No. 1, Issue 5, rev. ed., 1982) pp. 16-17.

14. See nearly any book by nearly any mystical, metaphysical, New Thought, or New Age author, from the Qabalah to Horace Quimby, Mary Baker Eddy, and the Fillmores to the newest works.

15. See, for example, Barbara Katz Rothman, "Who's Mom? Who's Dad? Who Knows ...": *New Directions for Women* (Jan./Feb., 1991), p. 4, as well as almost weekly news stories on gene technology.

16. See Tim (Otter) Zell, "Theagenesis: The Birth of the Goddess," delivered as a lecture, September, 1970; reprinted in *The Witches Broomstick*, Feb. 1972; excerpted in Dr. L.L. Martello's *Witchcraft, the Old Religion*, 1973; reprinted with annotations in *Green Egg*, May 1988. Zell's thesis predates Lovelock's work. See also an interesting

new book, Rupert Sheldrake's *Rebirth of Nature,* which seems to say that morphogenesis is a living process.

17. This is not solely a feminist issue. It also concerns African Americans and other non-European peoples. See, for example, Jerry Adler, et al., "African Dreams" and following articles and sidebars in *Newsweek* (Sept. 23, 1991), pp. 42-50.

18. For more on percussion, see the Appendix.

19. There are, of course, established systems of white and black magic, but my focus is on devotion, not on tradition or magic. For color magic, see, for example, *Real Magic* by Isaac Bonewits.

20. The best explication of these issues I've read is in Starhawk's *Truth or Dare.*

21. For example, see the many books on ritual in the Bibliography.

22. This chapter was originally written during the 1991 Gulf War, but the issues are always pertinent.

23. Helen's invocation is adapted, of course, from Starhawk's *The Spiral Dance.*

24. For information on drums, see the Appendix.

25. In general terms, ceremonial magic differs from what I do in that it is Judeo-Christian with borrowings from Egyptian mythology and Rosicrucianism. Ceremonial magic is extremely elaborate, using scripts, magical language, swords and other implements, and it has a highly hierarchical organization. One example is the Hermetic Order of the Golden Dawn, which was founded about 1890 and still exists in other forms.

26. See also the tables in the *Spiral Dance* and other books listed in the Bibliography.

27. The word "pagan" comes from the Latin *paganus,* which means country person. "Heathen" comes from the heath, the countryside.

28. See also Chapter 7.

29. Technically, we *invoke* powers "above" us and *evoke* powers "below" us. That is, we invoke angels and evoke elemental spirits.

30. There are many books that contain listings of the gods and goddesses and their festivals. See the Bibliography for details.

31. See the list of resources.

32. In the earlier versions of the story, Ninshubur is female, in later versions, male.

APPENDIX:
RAISING POWER
BY MAKING MUSIC

I've spent time in rituals with drums and in rituals without them, and I believe that while the human voice (sounding, chanting, or singing) is powerful alone, the power is increased geometrically if someone is beating a drum or shaking a rattle. There are rock paintings of women with drums, and it's easy to imagine early people beating on sticks, bones, or shells to keep time long before they learned to string guitars or hollow out flutes.

But the real power of drumming is the feeling you get, the energy you circulate. It echoes your pulse and magnifies it, it alters your consciousness, it thrusts you into the heartbeat and the dance of the Goddess herself. Alone or in a group, loud or soft, fast or slow, drumming sets up resonances in every cell of your body. It's a path to bliss.

Here, in order from simplest (and inexpensive) to fairly complex (and more expensive), is a list of percussion instruments you can use to raise power in your rituals.

1. **Clap your hands.** Slap your thighs. Tap your feet.

2. **Beat two sticks together.** You can buy beautiful hardwood sticks from instrument or folk music stores or two pieces of broomstick from a lumberyard. The best are Mexican *claves*, which have a musical tone because they're made of rosewood, ebony, and similar woods. Broomsticks are much less melodic, but they do make the rhythm. The sticks should be six inches to one foot in length.

3. **Shake a rattle.** You can buy elaborate gourd rattles or borrow your baby's plastic rattle. Instrument stores sell rattles from cultures around the world, in more shapes,

sizes, and materials than you can imagine. You can also make a "plain wrap" rattle out of a bottled water bottle (six-pack size). Be sure the bottle is completely dry inside, then pour in about a quarter cup (total) of a combination of popcorn, rice, dried beans, beads, and tiny shells. Shake the rattle, adjusting the amount and proportion of ingredients until the sound pleases you, then glue the cap on. Decorate the neck of the bottle with ribbons.

4. **Shake and tap a tambourine.** These, too, come in many sizes and prices. I've put ribbons through the finger hole of one tambourine and painted dancing figures around the rim of another one.

5. **Tip and shake a rainstick.** Rainsticks, which are usually made of bamboo, can be very expensive, but if you want one to use as a musical instrument, you need only a small one (two to three feet long). They're filled with beans and shells, and the rainfall sound is caused by the beans and shells falling against baffles inside the length of the stick. I have one large bamboo rainstick (four feet long) and two small rainsticks (three feet long and shorter, two inches or less in diameter). The small ones were made in Chile of dried Normata cactus filled with pebbles.

6. **Make anything into a musical instrument.** This follows the same principle as the found art I discussed in Chapter 2. Bells are good, as long as they're neither glass nor too shrill. You can shake them or tap them with a wood mallet. I know a woman who has turned a tin tea kettle into a drum, I've seen people beat rocks together, I know someone who raps her metal cheese grater with an old wooden spoon, and I've seen people use empty five-gallon water bottles as bass drums. Find something unbreakable and use your imagination.

7. **Beat a drum.** You'll find several kinds of drums in pagan rituals, from toy drums to hollowed-out tree trunks and conga drums. Here are three drums commonly used in pagan rituals:

- **Frame drums.** These may be the oldest. A frame drum's diameter is greater than its height. My drums, for example, are 10 by $3\frac{1}{2}$ inches and 12 by $2\frac{1}{2}$ inches, though frame drums come much smaller and much larger. Each of my drums has one head, with the leather fastenings gathered into a ring on the back. You can hold the drum by this ring or by a thong in the rim or rest it on your thigh while you strike it with a leather-tipped mallet or your fingertips. On Native American two-headed frame drums, one head (which has a slightly higher pitch) is named for Father Sky, and the other (which has a slightly lower pitch) is named for Mother Earth. Drumming patterns use one or both sides and sometimes set up dialogues between masculine and feminine energies. Traditionally, men have tended to use mallets and women their hands. I recommend that you use a mallet, especially if your frame drums are as small as mine, because you just can't make enough noise with your bare hands. I'm just learning to play a frame drum that looks like a tambourine. It's called a *rik* and comes from Egypt.

- **Tom-toms.** These are taller than they are round and vary in size from a few inches to the yards-wide drums that four men play together at Native American pow-wows. I've also seen two tom-toms made from one- or two-foot slices of hollowed-out tree trunks, which were smoked to dry them and then covered with skin heads. These drums have irregular shapes and mindboggling tones.

You can decorate frame drums and tom-toms with ribbons,

beads, feathers, shells, charms, etc., tied to the frame or paint designs on the heads. I've done both with no detriment to the tones of my drums.

- **Doumbeks.** These are especially popular with pagans and harmonize beautifully with the other percussion instruments. They are the womb-shaped drums you find in Middle Eastern belly-dancing orchestras. They're made of clay or hammered copper, brass, or nickel-plated tin and have skin or artificial membrane (mylar) heads. The high pops you may have heard from doumbeks are made by the clay (ceramic) doumbeks. While the tone of a clay doumbek is wonderful, the drums are, alas, breakable and sometimes heavy. My clay doumbek is fairly small (about ten inches tall with a seven-inch head) and glazed in silver, blue, and yellow; its voice is soprano. My brass doumbek is about fourteen inches tall with a ten-inch head; it's a tenor. I've decorated it with black ribbons and glittery tassels tied to the strap.

To play a doumbek, remove your rings and heavy, dangly bracelets so you don't ruin the head. Sit cross-legged and lean slightly forward. Cradle the drum across your left thigh and hold it gently in place with your left forearm. (Some of my friends who are very largely endowed hold their drum under their left breast.) Let the fingers of your left hand dangle over the edge of the head and tap one or two fingers on the head to make the high tones at the edge of the head, which are called "teks." Rest the heel of your right hand on the edge of the head about a quarter of the way around the circle. Your right hand moves back and forth into the center of the head, making teks on the edge and lower beats, which are called "doums," in the center of the head.

When you make quick, consecutive beats, left-right-left-right, it's called "tek-a-tek-a," the "a" being the rim tap with one or two fingers of your right hand.

There are innumerable traditional rhythms for the doumbek, and you could probably study a lifetime to master the instrument. But you don't have to. Pick a steady 4/4 or 3/4 beat, alternate hands, and jam.

Here are three basic rhythms, two of them relatively easy "beledi" rhythms, that you can play with. Practice very slowly and count aloud until the rhythm gets into your hands and becomes nearly automatic.

Begin with the "heartbeat" (or "mother") rhythm. Use two or three fingers of your right hand to slap doums in the middle of the head to the following count:

```
Count:  1     2     3    4     5     6    7    8
Stroke: Doum  doum  rest rest  doum  rest rest rest
Hand:   R     R                R
(repeat)
```

This is the beat you return to whenever you lose it while you're jamming; always listen for the doums, that is, and base yourself in them. When you feel confident (or bored) with this basic rhythm, add teks between the doums:

```
Count:  1     2      3 + 4        2      2 + 3 + 4
Stroke: Doum  DOUM   tek-a-tek    DOUM   tek-a-tek-a-tek
Hand:   R     R      R L R        R      R L R L R
(repeat)
```

```
Count:  1       2     3 + 4 +      1   2 + 3   4 +
Stroke: Doum DOUM tek-a-tek-a    doum tek-a-tek tek-a
Hand:   R       R    R L R L      R   R L R   R L
(repeat)
```

Don't be afraid to experiment with new rhythms and variations, and if you lose your rhythm, start counting your doums and teks until it comes back. You can also buy lesson books and tapes.

When you're drumming with a ritual, even by yourself, begin with the heartbeat (as Helen did in Chapter 4) and build up to louder, more complex rhythms as the cone of power builds. After you release the cone, gradually return to the heartbeat, which will also help ground you. You can do this with any percussion instrument. Enjoy!

BIBLIOGRAPHY

Absher, Tom. *Men and the Goddess: Feminine Archetypes in Western Literature*. Park Street Press, 1990.

Adler, Margot. *Drawing Down the Moon: Witches, Druids, Goddess-Worshippers, and Other Pagans in America Today*. Rev. ed. Beacon Press, 1986.

Allen, Paula Gunn. *Grandmothers of the Light: A Medicine Woman's Sourcebook*. Beacon Press, 1991.

Anderson, Lorraine, ed. *Sisters of the Earth: Women's Prose and Poetry about Nature*. Vintage Books, 1991.

Anderson, William. *Green Man: The Archetype of Our Oneness with the Earth*. HarperCollins, 1990.

Ardinger, Barbara, Ph.D. *Seeing Solutions*. New American Library, Signet New Age Book, 1989.

_____. *Granny Gosle's Tales*. Domina Mundi, 1994.

Ashcroft-Nowicki, Dolores. *First Steps in Ritual: Magical Techniques for Experiencing the Inner Worlds*. Aquarian Press, 1990.

Austin, Hallie Iglehart. *The Heart of the Goddess: Art, Myth and Meditations on the World's Sacred Feminine*. Wingbow Press, 1990.

Begg, Ean. *The Cult of the Black Virgin*. Arkana, 1985.

Berger, Pamela, *The Goddess Obscured: Transformations of the Grain Protectress from Goddess to Saint*. Beacon Press, 1985.

Bernal, Martin. *Black Athena: The Afroasiatic Roots of Classical Civilization*. Rutgers University Press, 1987.

Birnbaum, Lucia Chiavola. *Black Madonnas: Feminism, Religion, & Politics in Italy*. Northeastern University Press, 1993

Blair, Nancy. *The Amulets of the Goddess: Oracle of Ancient Wisdom*. Wingbow Press, 1993.

Bonewits, P.E.I. *Real Magic*. Creative Arts Book Co., 1971.

Brother Lawrence of the Resurrection. *The Practice of the Presence of God.* Ed. and trans. by John J. Delaney. Doubleday Image Book, 1977.

Broude, Norma and Mary D. Garrad, eds. *The Power of Feminist Art: The American Movement of the 1970s, History and Impact.* Abrams, 1994.

Budapest, Zsuzsanna. *The Grandmother of Time: A Woman's Book of Celebrations, Spells, and Sacred Objects for Every Month of the Year.* Harper & Row, 1989.

_____. *The Holy Book of Women's Mysteries.* 2 vols. Susan B. Anthony Coven No. 1, 1986.

Caldecott, Moyra. *Myths of the Sacred Tree.* Destiny Books, 1993.

Campanelli, Pauline. *The Wheel of the Year: Living the Magical Life.* Llewellyn, 1989.

_____. *Circles, Groves and Sanctuaries: Sacred Spaces of Today's Pagans.* Llewellyn, 1992.

Chernin, Kim. *Reinventing Eve: Modern Woman in Search of Herself.* Times Books, 1987.

Christ, Carol P. *Laughter of Aphrodite: Reflections on a Journey to the Goddess.* Harper & Row, 1987.

Clifton, Chas. S., ed. *Witchcraft and Shamanism. Book 3, Witchcraft Today.* Llewellyn, 1994.

Cooper, J.C. *The Aquarian Dictionary of Festivals.* Aquarian Press, 1990.

Crawford, O.G.S. *The Eye Goddesses.* Delphi Press, 1991.

Cunningham, Scott. *Cunningham's Encyclopedia of Crystal, Gem, and Metal Magic.* Llewellyn, 1988.

_____. *Cunningham's Encyclopedia of Magical Herbs.* Llewellyn, 1988.

_____. *Wicca: A Guide for the Solitary Practitioner.* Llewellyn, 1988.

Daly, Mary. *Gyn/Ecology: The Metaethics of Radical Feminism.* Beacon Press, 1978.

_____ and Jane Caputi. *Webster's First New Intergalactic Wickedary of the English Language*. Beacon Press, 1987.

Denning, Melita and Osborne Phillips. *The Magical Philosophy*. 5 vols. Llewellyn, 1974–82.

Dexter, Miriam Robbins. *Whence the Goddesses: A Source Book*. Pergamon Press, Athene Series, 1990.

Diamond, Irene and Gloria Feman Orenstein. *Reweaving the World: The Emergence of Ecofeminism*. Sierra Club Books, 1990.

Durdin-Robertson, Lawrence. *The Year of the Goddess: A Perpetual Calendar of Festivals*. Aquarian Press, 1990.

Edwards, Betty. *Drawing on the Right Side of the Brain*. J.P. Tarcher, 1979.

Eisler, Riane. *The Chalice and the Blade: Our History, Our Future*. Harper & Row, 1987.

Eller, Cynthia. *Living in the Lap of the Goddess: The Feminist Spirituality Movement in America*. Crossroad, 1993.

Farrar, Janet & Stewart. *Eight Sabbats for Witches*. Phoenix, 1981.

_____. *The Witches' God*. Phoenix, 1989.

_____. *The Witches' Goddess*. Phoenix, 1987.

Farrar, Stewart. *What Witches Do*. Phoenix, 1983.

Fitch, Ed. *Magical Rites from the Crystal Well*. Llewellyn, 1986.

Fox, Matthew. *Original Blessing: A Primer in Creation Spirituality*. Bear & Company, 1983.

Gadon, Elinor W. *The Once and Future Goddess*. Harper & Row, 1989.

Galland, China. *Longing for Darkness: Tara and the Black Madonna*. Viking, 1990.

Gardner, Gerald. *Witchcraft Today*. Magickal Childe, 1988.

George, Demetra. *Mysteries of the Dark Moon: The Healing Powers of the Dark Goddess*. HarperSanFrancisco, 1992.

Gimbutas, Marija. *The Civilization of the Goddess: The World of Old Europe.* HarperSanFrancisco, 1991.

_____. *The Goddesses and Gods of Old Europe.* University of California Press, 1982.

_____. *The Language of the Goddess.* Harper & Row, 1989.

Ginzburg, Carlo. *Ecstacies: Deciphering the Witches' Sabbath.* Trans. Raymond Rosenthal. Penguin Books, 1991.

Gleason, Judith. *Oya: In Praise of the Goddess.* Shambhala, 1987.

Gleick, James. *Chaos: Making a New Science.* Penguin, 1987.

Gonzales-Wippler, Migene. *The Complete Book of Spells, Ceremonies and Magic.* Llewellyn, 1988.

Goodrich, Normal Lorre. *Priestesses.* Franklin Watts, 1989.

Gordon, Stuart. *The Encyclopedia of Myths and Legends.* Trafalgar Square, 1993.

Gottner-Abendroth, Heide. *The Dancing Goddess: Principles of a Matriarchal Aesthetic.* Trans. Maureen T. Krause. Beacon Press, 1991.

Grey, Morgan and Julia Penelope. *Found Goddesses, Asphalta to Viscera.* New Victoria Publishers, 1988.

Griffin, Susan. *Woman and Nature: The Roaring Inside Her.* Harper & Row, 1978.

Hart, Mickey, with Jay Stevens. *Drumming at the Edge of Magic: A Journey Into the Spirit of Percussion.* HarperSanFrancisco, 1990.

Hirschfield, Jane, ed. *Women in Praise of the Sacred: 43 Centuries of Spiritual Poetry by Women.* HarperCollins, 1994.

Johnson, Buffie. *Lady of the Beasts: Ancient Images of the Goddess and Her Animals.* Harper & Row, 1988.

Jong, Erica. *Witches.* Abrams, 1981.

Judith, Anodea. *Wheels of Life: A User's Guide to the Chakra System.* Llewellyn, 1988.

_____, and Selene Vega. *The Sevenfold Journey: Reclaiming Mind, Body & Spirit Through the Chakras.* Crossing Press, 1993.

Karas, Sheryl Ann. *The Solstice Evergreen: The History, Folklore and Origin of the Christmas Tree.* Aslan Publishing, 1991.

Katzeff, Paul. *Full Moons: Fact & Fantasy About Lunar Influence.* Citadel Press, 1981.

Keirsey, David and Marilyn Bates. *Please Understand Me: Character and Temperament Types.* Prometheus Nemesis Books, 1978.

Kraig, Donald Michael. *Modern Magick: Eleven Lessons in the High Magickal Arts.* Llewellyn, 1988.

Kurenga, Maulana. *The African American Holiday of Kwanzaa: A Celebration of Family, Community, and Culture.* University of Sankore Press, 1989.

Laura, Judith. *She Lives! The Return of Our Great Mother: Myths, Rituals, Meditations, & Music.* Crossing Press, 1990.

Lauter, Estella. *Women as Mythmakers: Poetry and Visual Art by Twentieth-Century Women.* Indiana University Press, 1984.

Loudon, Jennifer. *The Woman's Comfort Book: A Self-Nurturing Guide for Restoring Balance in Your Life.* HarperSanFrancisco, 1992.

Lovelock, James. *The Ages of Gaia: A Biography of Our Living Earth.* Norton, 1988.

Martello, Leo Louis. *Witchcraft: The Old Religion.* Citadel Press, n.d.

McCrickard, Janet. *Eclipse of the Sun: An Investigation Into Sun and Moon Myths.* Gothic Image Publications, 1990.

Monaghan, Patricia. *The Book of Goddesses and Heroines.* Llewellyn, 1990.

_____. *O Mother Sun! A New View of the Cosmic Feminine.* Crossing Press, 1994.

Mutén, Burleigh, ed. *The Return of the Great Goddess.* Shambhala, 1994.

Neuman, Erich. *The Great Mother: An Analysis of the Archetype.* Trans. Ralph Manheim. Princeton University Press,

Bollingen Series XLVII, 1972.

Noble, Vicki. *Motherpeace: A Way to the Goddess Through Myth, Art, and Tarot.* Harper & Row, 1983.

____. *Shakti Woman: Feeling Our Fire, Healing Our World.* Harper-SanFrancisco, 1991.

____, ed. *Uncoiling the Snake: Ancient Patterns in Contemporary Women's Lives.* HarperSanFrancisco, 1993.

Orenstein, Gloria Feman. *The Reflowering of the Goddess.* Pergamon Press, Athene Series, 1990.

Pagels, Elaine. *The Gnostic Gospels.* Random House, 1979.

Parrish-Harra, Carol E. *The Book of Rituals: Personal and Planetary Transformation.* IBS Press, 1990.

Ranke-Heinemann, Uta. *Eunuchs for the Kingdom of Heaven: Women, Sexuality, and the Catholic Church.* Trans. Peter Heinegg. Doubleday, 1990.

Renee, Janina. *Tarot Spells.* Llewellyn, 1990.

Robert, Elizabeth and Elias Amidon. *Earth Prayers: 365 Prayers, Poems, & Invocations for Honoring the Earth.* HarperSanFrancisco, 1991.

Rose, Jeanne. *Herbs & Things.* Putnam Perigee Book, 1972.

Rush, Anne Kent. *Moon, Moon.* Random House, 1976.

Sheldrake, Rupert. *The Rebirth of Nature: The Greening of Science and God.* Bantam Books, 1991.

Shepherd, Linda Jean, Ph.D. *Lifting the Veil: The Feminine Face of Science.* Shambhala, 1993.

Sjöö, Monica and Barbara Mor. *The Great Cosmic Mother: Rediscovering the Religion of the Earth.* Harper & Row, 1987.

Spretnak, Charlene. *Lost Goddesses of Early Greece: A Collection of Pre-Hellenic Myths.* Beacon Press, 1978.

____. *The Spiritual Dimension of Green Politics.* Bear & Company, 1986.

Starhawk. *The Spiral Dance: A Rebirth of the Ancient Religion of the Great Goddess.* Rev. ed. Harper & Row, 1989.

_____. *Truth or Dare: Encounters with Power, Authority, and Mystery.* Harper & Row, 1987.

Stein, Diane. *Casting the Circle: A Women's Book of Ritual.* Crossing Press, 1990.

_____. *The Goddess Book of Days: A Perpetual 366 Day Engagement Calendar.* Llewellyn, 1988.

Stepanich, Kisma K. *The Gaia Tradition: Celebrating the Earth in Her Seasons.* Llewellyn, 1991.

Stone, Merlin, *When God Was a Woman.* Harcourt Brace Jovanovich, 1976.

Streep, Peg. *Sanctuaries of the Goddess: The Sacred Landscapes and Objects.* Bulfinch Press, 1994.

Teish, Luisah. *Jambalaya: The Natural Woman's Book.* Harper & Row, 1985.

Teubal, Savina J. *Sarah the Priestess: The First Matriarch of Genesis.* Swallow Press, 1986.

Thompson, William Irwin. *The Time Falling Bodies Take to Light: Mythology, Sexuality and the Origins of Culture.* St. Martin's Press, 1981.

Valiente, Doreen. *An ABC of Witchcraft.* Phoenix, 1973.

_____. *Witchcraft for Tomorrow.* Phoenix, 1978.

Vare, Ethlie Ann and Greg Ptack. *Mothers of Invention: From the Bra to the Bomb.* Morrow, 1988.

Walker, Barbara G. *The Crone: Woman of Age, Wisdom, & Power.* Harper & Row, 1985.

_____. *The Secrets of the Tarot.* Harper & Row, 1984.

_____. *The Woman's Dictionary of Symbols and Sacred Objects.* Harper & Row, 1988.

_____. *The Woman's Encyclopedia of Myths and Secrets.* Harper & Row, 1983.

Weed, Susan S. *Menopausal Years: A Wise Woman's Way.* Ash Tree Publishing, 1992.

Weinstein, Marion. *Positive Magic: Occult Self-Help*. Phoenix, 1981.

Wilber, Ken. *The Spectrum of Consciousness*. Theosophical Publishing House, Quest Book, 1979.

Wilshire, Donna. *Virgin Mother Crone: Myths & Mysteries of the Triple Goddess*. Inner Traditions, 1994.

Woolger, Jennifer Barker & Roger S. *The Goddess Within: A Guide to the Eternal Myths that Shape Women's Lives*. Fawcett Columbine, 1989.

Wynne, Patrice. *The Womanspirit Sourcebook: A Catalog of Books, Periodicals, Music, Calendars and Tarot Cards, Organizations, Video and Audio Tapes, Bookstores, Interviews, Meditations, Art*. Harper & Row, 1988.

Zalewski, Patrick J. *Secret Inner Order Rituals of the Golden Dawn, with the Approval of Israel Regardie*. Ed. by Joseph Lisiewski. Falcon Press, 1988.

Zukav, Gary. *The Dancing Wu Li Masters: An Overview of the New Physics*. Morrow, 1979.

RESOURCES

Amnesty International monthly "Urgent Action" letter-writing campaigns on behalf of prisoners of conscience: if your local NPR station doesn't broadcast AI Reports, write to KCRW-FM, 1900 Pico Blvd., Santa Monica, CA 90405, or phone 310/450-5183 for information. It's free.

Candles, oils, herbs: you can purchase all of these (and more) by mail from The Eye of the Cat, 3314 East Broadway, Long Beach, CA 90803. Write for a catalog.

Look in the ad sections of the periodicals listed below for additional resources, also in your local Yellow Pages. You can find these supplies at botanicas and craft fairs, renaissance fairs, and similar events.

You can also buy candles at your local grocery store. Most of the herbs I use come out of my kitchen cabinet.

Goddess jewelry: available at metaphysical bookstores. Also write to these sources for catalogs:

- Ancient Circles, P.O. Box 787, Laytonville, GA 95454.
- Beltane Bookstore, P.O. Box 8, Clear Lake, WA 98235.
- Church of All Worlds/Nemeton, P.O. Box 1542, Ukiah, CA 94709.
- Star River Productions, P.O. Box 6254, North Brunswick, NJ 08902.

Most of these sources also sell goddess images.

Lunar calendar: available at your local bookstore or from Luna Press, P.O. Box 511, Kenmore Station, Boston, MA 02215.

Mailing lists: pick up one or more of the periodicals listed below at your local metaphysical bookstore or write for current subscription information:

- *Circle Network News*, P.O. Box 219, Mt. Horeb, WI 53572.
- *Creation Spirituality*, P.O. Box 19216, Oakland, CA 94619. Based on Matthew Fox's *Creation Spirituality*.
- *Green Egg, A Journal of The Awakening Earth*, P.O. Box 1542, Ukiah, CA 95482.
- *New Directions for Women*, 108 W. Palisade Ave., Englewood, NJ 07631. Both political and spiritual.
- *Of a Like Mind*, P.O. Box 6021, Madison, WI 53716.
- *SageWoman Magazine*, P.O. Box 641, Point Arena, CA 95468.
- *Woman of Power*, P.O. Box 2785, Orleans, MA 02653.

For other periodicals, see the classified and display ads in these magazines; you'll find something to meet your every need.

Musical Instruments: My favorite store in the whole world is the Folk Music Center, 220 Yale Ave., Claremont, CA 91711. Write for information on specific instruments.

In your local area, look for drums and other instruments in musical instrument stores, pawn shops, craft and renaissance fairs, and ethnic festivals.

DISCOGRAPHY

You can find wonderful music on tape and CD in the New Age section of your local record stores or in metaphysical bookstores. Also check the Ladyslipper and Gaia Bookstore catalogs, the Womanspirit Sourcebook, and ads in the periodicals listed earlier. Use any kind of music that appeals to you, from Mozart to the Grateful Dead, from Sweet Honey in the Rock to Phillip Glass.

Here is a list of a few of my favorites:

Almeida, Laurindo, et al. *Duets with the Spanish Guitar.* Angel. 4XS-36050.

Barrett, Ruth and Felicity Artemis Flowers. *Invocation to Free Women.* Circle of Aradia Publications, P.O. Box 1608, Topanga, CA 90290. Be sure to listen to Ruth's more recent recordings.

Benoit, Bernard, et al. *Lutunn Noz, Celtic Music for Guitar.* Musical Heritage Society. MHC 5577.

Britten, Benjamin. *A Ceremony of Carols* (many versions).

Ciani, Suzanne. *History of My Heart.* Private Music, Inc.

_____. *The Velocity of Love.* RCA.

Evenson, Dean. *Ocean Dreams.* Soundings of the Planet, P.O. Box 43512, Tucson, AZ 85733.

Fitzgerald, Scott. *Thunderdrums.* Nature Recordings, P.O. Box 2749, Friday Harbor, WA 98250, 800/228-5711.

Gardner, Kay. *Mooncircles.* Ladyslipper. Be sure to listen to all of Kay's recordings.

Gass, Robert and On Wings of Song. *From the Goddess.* Spring Hill Music, 5216 Sunshine Canyon, Boulder, CO 80302.

_____. *Ancient Mother.* Spring Hill Music.

Hart, Mickey, et al. *At the Edge.* Rykodisc.

Holst, Gustave. *The Planets.* Many versions available, including electronic fantasies; find the one you like.

Libana. *A Circle Is Cast.* Libana, Inc., P.O. Box 530, Cambridge, MA 02140. A songbook is also available.

___. *Fire Within.* Libana, Inc.

Light Rain. *Dream Dancer.* Magi Productions, P.O. Box 356, Larkspur, CA 94939.

Murphy, Charlie. *Catch the Fire.* Good Fairy Productions, P.O. Box 12188, Broadway Sta., Seattle, WA 98102.

Ortiz, Alfredo Rolando. *Harp for Quiet Moments.* A.R. Ortiz, P.O. Box 911, Corona, CA 91718.

Pinner, Sue Ann. *Ave Maria.* VQR Distal. On side 1 are 10 different *Ave Marias.*

Roth, Gabrielle. *Ritual.* Raven Recordings, P.O. Box 2034, Red Bank, NJ 07701. Be sure to listen to her other recordings.

Thiel, Lisa. *Songs of the Spirit.* Sacred Dream Productions, P.O. Box 931424, Los Angeles, CA 90093. Be sure to listen to her other recordings.

VonBingen, Hildegard. *Ordo Virtutum.* Deutche Harmonia Mundi.

ABOUT THE AUTHOR

Barbara Ardinger, M.A., Ph.D., has worked as a technical writer/editor in five different industries, taught both sacred and secular classes to adults, and has been a freelance writer since 1983. Born in St. Louis and a resident of Southern California since 1976, she writes a regular column for an Orange County business magazine and articles and book reviews for national magazines. Her first book, *Seeing Solutions*, was published in 1989; in 1994, she published *Granny Gosle's Tales*, a book of revisionist fairy tales. She has three Goddess novels in progress.

She "came out of the broomcloset" several years ago. In addition to Goddess lore, she has studied Tarot, meditation, numerology, color, psychic healing, the Quabalah, and the Aramaic origins of the Bible. She has been initiated into an occult order, is a member of the Fellowship of Isis, and has been a member of three covens. Currently she is a happy solitary, though she gets around.

Since her son, who is a poet, has grown up and left home, she lives quietly with her two cats, Schroedinger and Heisenberg, in an abundance of books and goddesses and treasures.

New World Library is dedicated to publishing books
and cassettes that help improve the quality of our lives.

For a catalog of our fine books and cassettes, contact:

NEW WORLD LIBRARY
14 Pamaron Way
Novato, CA 94949
Phone: (415) 884–2100
Fax: (415) 884–2199

Or call toll-free: (800) 227–3900